THE NEW
Students' Veggie
COOKBOOK

THE NEW
Students' Veggie
COOKBOOK

Carolyn Humphries

foulsham

LONDON • NEW YORK • TORONTO • SYDNEY

foulsham

The Oriel, Thames Valley Court, 183–187 Bath Road,
Slough, Berkshire, SL1 4AA, England

Foulsham books can be found in all good bookshops and direct from www.foulsham.com

ISBN: 978-0-572-03522-8

Copyright © 2009 W. Foulsham & Co. Ltd

Cover photographs © Superstock and Istock

A CIP record for this book is available from the British Library

The moral right of the author has been asserted

All rights reserved

The Copyright Act prohibits (subject to certain very limited exceptions) the making of
copies of any copyright work or of a substantial part of such a work, including the
making of copies by photocopying or similar process. Written permission to make a copy
or copies must therefore normally be obtained from the publisher in advance. It is
advisable also to consult the publisher if in any doubt as to the legality of any copying
which is to be undertaken.

Printed in Great Britain by Printwise (Haverhill) Ltd, Haverhill

Contents

Starting out

Leaving home for college or university is probably one of the biggest steps you'll take in life. Your first taste of real freedom where you are responsible for you – totally. The problem is, looking after yourself on a daily basis can be a bit of a drag if you don't get your act together. Thinking about shopping and cooking as well as enjoying a great social life (and, of course, studying) is a lot to cope with.

This book is designed for anyone who hasn't had to cook for themselves before. It won't insult you by telling you how to open a can of baked beans and put them on toast (mind you, that's a great standby when you're short of time and money) but it does have masses of really tasty, nourishing meals that don't cost a fortune, are dead simple and don't take ages to prepare.

One of the advantages of being vegetarian is that you can often eat more cheaply than if you include meat in your diet. The book also has loads of advice on what to eat to keep fit and well and how to cook the basics – such as vegetables, pulses, pasta, rice and eggs. It has simple ways to make meals go further if you have friends round, food to eat to keep you going during exams and tasty snacks that can easily be turned into main meals to eke out the last few quid for the term. Most of the dishes serve two so, if you are eating on your own, you've enough for two days but, if you prefer, most of the recipes can be halved easily. There's also a simple guide to what you'll need to buy to set up a useful storecupboard from which you can make quick and easy meals, and also basic food hygiene.

What you eat is important

To enjoy life to the full (and to help the brain cells work), a healthy diet is vital. You need a balance made up of the following food groups:

- At least five portions of fruit and vegetables a day (that doesn't include potatoes). You need them for vitamins, minerals and general well-being. Many are also cheap, which helps a lot. Eat them cooked or raw, canned, frozen or fresh.

TIP: Market stalls are likely to be cheaper than the supermarket for fresh produce. If you are buying in a supermarket look for economy ranges or buy loose rather than pre-packed – it's cheaper and better for the environment.

- Loads of starchy foods (complex carbohydrates) for energy and to fill you up. At least half of what you eat should come from foods like bread, potatoes, rice, pasta and breakfast cereals (wholegrain varieties such as muesli, porridge, Weetabix or Shredded Wheat rather than sugary ones). They provide slow-release energy to keep you sustained both in body and mind!

TIP: Buy supermarket own brands – they're much cheaper.

- At least two portions of protein a day for body growth and repair. As you are not going to eat meat or fish, you must get yours from pulses (dried peas, beans and lentils, including baked beans), eggs, dairy products like cheese, milk and yoghurt (or soya alternatives if you are vegan), nuts and vegetable proteins like tofu or TVP (soya mince or chunks). I haven't used Quorn in the recipes because it's comparatively expensive but you can substitute it for any of the soya mince recipes, bearing in mind that 50 g/½ mug dry soy mince is equivalent to about 175 g /generous mug of Quorn mince.

- A very little fat – essential for body warmth and energy, BUT you don't need masses of extra butter or margarine or loads of oil for frying. You get most of what you need naturally in other foods, such as dairy products, nuts and cereals, so have only a scraping of butter or margarine on bread, use the minimum of oil for cooking (drain well before eating) and try to grill rather than deep-fry foods where possible.

TIP: Avoid too many takeaways and ready meals. Not only are they expensive, they're also high in fat, salt and sugar.

Setting up your kitchen

Most furnished accommodation supplies basic kitchen equipment. All being well this will include a cooker with an oven and a fridge with either a freezer or freezing compartment. Most students need to take their own crockery and cutlery, tea towels and washing up cloths.

For cooking utensils, you don't need much and you certainly don't need gadgets.

- Bowls – including one that's microwave safe and big enough for mixing as well as tasks like scrambling eggs
- Chopping board
- Colander or large sieve for straining cooked vegetables, pasta or rice
- Draining spoon, long-handled, with holes in it
- Fish slice for lifting foods out of a frying pan or from a baking sheet
- Frying pan
- Grater
- Kettle and toaster (You could wait until you get to where you're staying as you may find everyone has them and you won't need to buy your own)
- Kitchen scissors
- Knives – vegetable knife and bread knife
- Oven gloves
- Ovenproof dish
- Paperware – kitchen paper, foil and/or clingfilm
- Potato masher (use a fork if you don't have one)
- Potato peeler (easier than a vegetable knife)
- Roasting tins
- Saucepans, ideally one small, one medium and one large, with lids
- Whisk – a balloon or wire one is ideal for making sauces and combining ingredients
- Wooden spoon

Your first basic shop

If you're lucky, your parents will be keen to buy a box of essentials to take with you (so they know you can survive the first few days). If you give them this list, it'll help with ideas for the basics for everyday life and a few of the mainstay store cupboard ingredients you'll often need for cooking the recipes in this book.

Basic cupboard fodder

- Cereal – wholegrain is better than sugary; it'll fill you up and give you energy for longer
- Curry powder or curry paste
- Garlic – a tub or jar is much easier than fiddling around crushing cloves – store in the fridge once opened
- Herbs – dried mixed herbs are good for flavouring lots of savoury dishes but if you are more adventurous you might add dried oregano, basil, mint and sage
- Honey – good for sweetening and on toast
- Marmalade, jam or Marmite or other yeast extract for toast
- Mayonnaise or salad cream
- Milk powder or long-life milk – for when you run out of fresh

- Oil – sunflower, vegetable or olive
- Parmesan style cheese – a tub of dried, grated hard cheese, suitable for vegetarians
- Pasta
- Plain flour, plus self-raising if you plan to do any baking
- Raisins or sultanas – good for snacking, on cereals and in lots of recipes
- Rice – long-grain
- Salt and pepper – preferably buy a mill filled with black peppercorns
- Sauces – tomato ketchup, brown and soy sauces
- Spices – chilli powder and ground cinnamon to start
- Stock cubes – vegetable
- Sugar – caster is fine for most uses
- Tea and coffee
- Tomato purée – a tube is easiest – store in fridge once opened
- Vinegar – white wine will do for anything

Cans

- Tomatoes – economy brands are fine, and whole are cheaper than ready chopped (just crush up with a wooden spoon when you add them)
- Baked beans
- Red kidney beans
- Sweetcorn

In the fridge

- Bread – it'll keep longer in the fridge
- Butter or margarine
- Cheddar cheese – choose a strong-flavoured one, if you like it, then you don't need to use so much in cooking
- Eggs
- Milk – keep a carton in the freezer so you won't run out; it does take ages to thaw though, and will need a good shake once defrosted

Making the basics

The old expression 'He can't even boil an egg' isn't so funny – many people can't! Here are some simple instructions for all the basic foods you'll want to cook.

Eggs

Boiled: Place the eggs in a small saucepan and just cover with cold water. Cover with a lid (for quicker boiling) and bring to the boil. As soon as the water boils, start your timer and cook for $3\frac{1}{2}$ minutes for runny yolks and firm whites, 5–6 minutes for hard-boiled.

TIP: An egg pricker, which you can buy in hardware shops, is a great little gadget. You pierce the air sac end of the egg and it prevents it cracking when boiling.

TIP: For hard-boiled eggs to eat cold, plunge them immediately into cold water and shell them quickly after cooking to stop that black ring forming round the yolks.

Fried: Heat a very little oil in a frying pan. Break each egg into a cup and gently slide into the hot oil. Spoon a little oil over the eggs as they fry and remove with a fish slice as soon as they are cooked how you like them.

Poached: Bring a frying pan of water to the boil and then turn down the heat until there are just tiny bubbles. Add 1 tbsp of vinegar or lemon juice. Break each egg into a cup, then gently slide into the simmering water. Cook for 3 minutes for soft yolks, 4–5 minutes for hard. Do not boil rapidly or the white will break up. Lift out with a fish slice. Use very fresh eggs.

Scrambled: Heat a knob of butter or margarine and 1 tbsp of milk for each egg in a saucepan. Whisk in the eggs with a whisk or a fork. When well blended, add a little salt and pepper and cook over a gentle heat, stirring all the time until the mixture scrambles but is still creamy. Do not allow it to boil or it will go rubbery and watery. Serve immediately and soak the pan in hot soapy water straight away or it will be horrible to clean!

Omelette: See page 149.

Potatoes

Boiled: Peel or scrub and cut into even-sized pieces. Place in a pan with just enough cold water to cover. Add a pinch of salt, if you like. Part-cover with a lid, bring to the boil, reduce the heat slightly and boil quickly until tender (about 10 minutes, depending on the size of the pieces). Drain.

TIP: When a sharp knife slides easily into the potatoes, they are ready.

Chips: Oven chips are the easiest option, and to save fuel you can also cook them in the grill pan under a moderate grill instead of in the oven, but do keep turning them and watch carefully as they burn easily. Not quite as satisfying and more-ish as the real thing, though, is it? So, here's how it's done.

Peel, if you like, and cut each potato into finger-thick slices. Then cut each slice into chips. Pat dry on kitchen paper or on a clean tea towel. Heat enough oil to three-quarters fill the frying pan, or at least 2.5 cm/1 in in a saucepan (or use a chip pan if you have one). To test the temperature, slide in one chip down the back of the fish slice into the oil. If it starts to sizzle immediately, the oil is ready. Gently slide the chips down the fish slice into the pan a handful at a time, and spread then out with the slice. Cook until golden and soft in the centre. Drain on kitchen paper before serving.

TIP: Don't add more chips than the pan will hold comfortably – if they are packed in and sticking out of the oil the temperature will drop too much and they will stew rather than fry crisply. Better to cook two batches if necessary.

Jacket-baked: Scrub, leave whole and prick a few times with a fork. Rub with oil and salt (if you like) and place directly on the middle shelf of the oven. Bake at 180°C/350°F/gas 4/fan oven 160°C for about 1 hour or until the potatoes feel soft when squeezed with an oven-gloved hand. The oven temperature isn't vital; cook for longer in a slower oven for best taste, or for a shorter time in a hotter oven.

TIP: If you thread the potatoes on to metal skewers they will cook more quickly. Don't put on an oven for just one or two potatoes – it's a waste of fuel, for which read money.

If you have a microwave, prick the potatoes, wrap in kitchen paper and microwave for about 4 minutes per potato until soft when squeezed. Leave to stand for a few minutes before eating. They taste better if you crisp the skins under a hot grill for a few minutes.

Mashed: Peel first and prepare as for boiled. Once cooked and drained, add a knob of butter or margarine and a dash of milk. Mash with a potato masher or fork until smooth, then beat briefly until fluffy. You can add a little more milk or butter if it doesn't look creamy enough.

Roast: Peel or scrub and cut into even-sized pieces. Place in a pan and just cover with water. Add a pinch of salt, part-cover with a lid, bring to the boil and cook for about 3 minutes. Drain off the water. Cover firmly with the lid and, holding the lid on, give the pan a really good shake to roughen the edges of the potatoes. Meanwhile, heat a little oil in a roasting tin in the oven at 190°C/375°F/gas 5/fan oven 170°C until sizzling. Add the potatoes (careful – they will spit). Turn over in the oil then roast at the top of the oven for about 1 hour, turning once or twice during the cooking time, until crisp and golden.

Sautéed: Cut into small pieces or dice. Heat a little oil (or half butter or margarine, half oil) in a frying pan and fry, turning, until golden brown and cooked through – about 7 minutes, depending on the size. Add a little garlic towards the end of cooking, if you like. Drain on kitchen paper before serving.

TIP: Courgettes are great cooked this way too and they'll cook a bit quicker.

Carrots and other root vegetables

Boiled: Peel or scrub, then slice or cut into fingers. Place in a pan with just enough cold water to cover. Add a pinch of salt, if you like. Part-cover with a lid, bring to the boil, reduce the heat slightly and boil quickly until just tender (about 6 minutes, depending on the size of the pieces). Drain.

Roast: Peel and cut in even-sized pieces. No need to par-boil unless you're cooking potatoes too. Toss in oil in a baking tin and roast as for potatoes.

Green vegetables

Boiled: Shred or tear leafy ones, separate broccoli or cauliflower into small florets, top and tail beans or mangetout, top, tail and slice runner beans, shell peas or broad beans. Bring a little lightly salted water to the boil, add the vegetables, push down in the boiling water, cover and boil rapidly until just tender, no longer – usually just a few minutes. Drain (use the liquid for gravy or sauce if possible) and serve.

Steamed: Prepare your veg as above but place in a metal colander over a pan of boiling water. Cover with a lid and steam until just tender – again, just 5–8 minutes. Don't put too many in the colander at one time, and allow a little longer than for boiling. Don't overcook or they will lose their colour and nutrients.

Frozen veg: Peas are a great stand-by but bags of loose frozen veg – like broccoli or cauliflower – also save waste and help you get your five a day. Just tip them frozen into a pan of rapidly boiling water, turn the heat up high to bring back to the boil as quickly as possible, then boil for a couple of minutes until just tender.

Mixed vegetables – and other things

Stir-fried: This is a way of cooking vegetables quickly so they stay crunchy and delicious. Cut into thin strips as near the same size as possible so they cook evenly. Heat a little oil in a wok or frying pan until really hot. Add the vegetables and stir over a high heat, so they mix and cook evenly, for a few minutes until cooked to your liking. The vegetables should still be slightly crunchy.

Rice

Boiled: Rinse and drain the rice. Bring a large pan of lightly salted water to the boil, add the rice, stir, then boil rapidly for 10 minutes (or according to packet directions) until the rice is tender but the grains are still separate. Strain in a colander and pour some boiling water over to rinse off any excess starch, then drain again.

TIP: One serving is about 2 handfuls or $\frac{1}{4}$ mug of uncooked rice.

Oven-baked: Use 1 measure of rice and $2\frac{1}{2}$ times as much salted water or stock so, for 4 people, use a mug of rice and $2\frac{1}{2}$ mugs of liquid. Melt a knob of butter or margarine in a flameproof dish, then stir in the rice. Add the stock or water and bring to the boil. Cover with foil or a lid and place in the oven at 180°C/350°F/gas 4/fan oven 160°C. Cook for 20 minutes or until the rice is tender and has absorbed all the liquid. Don't overcook or it will go mushy.

TIP: Ovenproof means it goes in the oven – like Pyrex – flameproof means you can use it on the hob. If in doubt, use a saucepan on the hob.

Steamed: Use the same quantities as for oven-baked rice. Rinse the rice and put it in a pan. Cover with the liquid and bring just to the boil. Cover with a piece of foil, then a tight-fitting lid. Turn down the heat as low as possible and cook for 15 minutes. Keep the lid on. Turn off the heat and leave to stand for just 5 minutes, then remove the cover and fluff up with a fork.

Pasta

Bring plenty of lightly salted water to the boil. Add the pasta and bring back to the boil. Add 1 tbsp oil to prevent it boiling over, then boil rapidly, uncovered, for 10 minutes (or according to the packet directions), stirring occasionally to prevent sticking, until the pasta is just tender but still with a little 'bite'. Drain and use as required.

TIPS: Allow about 75 g/3 oz (2-3 large handfuls) raw pasta shapes or ⅙-¼ x 500g packet spaghetti (depending on appetites). For spaghetti, bring the water to the boil, then stand the spaghetti in the water and gently push down so the spaghetti curls round in the pan as it softens in the boiling water. For small pasta like macaroni, you only need about 50g/2oz (2 handfuls) per person.

And that means what?

Once you start to get interested in cooking and you look at more recipes, you'll come across cookery terms that may be unfamiliar. If you haven't come across them watching Gordon or Jamie, here's what they mean.

Beat: Tilt the bowl of ingredients in one hand and stir round fast and firmly in one direction with a wooden spoon. Keep going until it's smooth.

TIP: To chop fresh herbs, put them in a mug and snip with scissors.

Chop: Cut any vegetable or fruit in half first so the flat cut side is down on the chopping board. Then hold firmly in one hand and, using a sharp knife, make cuts at even distances along the length of the food not quite through one end. Then, still holding it together, make cuts across it so that it is cut into small pieces. To chop finely, simply make the cuts closer together; to chop coarsely … you don't need me to tell you.

TIP: If you hate chopping onions, buy a bag of frozen, diced onion and use a handful instead.

Dice: Much like chopping but into bigger cubes and you can cut right through the food at both ends as it's easier to hold together.

Flameproof: This is not the same as 'ovenproof' but means anything that can go on the hob or under the grill as well. If in doubt – about a casserole dish that you want to use under the grill, for example – don't.

Fold: This is like mixing lightly to keep air in a mixture. Use a metal spoon and gently cut and turn over the mixture using a figure-of-eight motion.

Grate: Hold the grater firmly in one hand over a plate and rub the ingredient to be grated up and down the appropriate side of the grater. Use the different sides to grate coarsely for cheese, carrots or chocolate, medium for lemon rind, or finely for nutmeg.

Knead: Gently work the mixture – usually dough – together to a ball with your hands, then put it on a board and squeeze and press until it forms a ball without any cracks. For bread you hold it with one hand, use the heel of the other to stretch the dough away from you then fold it back over itself. Keep repeating the process until it is smooth and elastic.

Mash: Use a potato masher or fork. Press the ingredient against the sides of the bowl or saucepan so it is forced through the gaps in the fork or masher to form a smoothish paste.

TIP: For potatoes or other cooked veg add a knob of butter or margarine and give them a good beat with the masher or a wooden spoon once mashed to make them fluffy.

Pare: Cut thin shreds of rind off something with a small, sharp knife.

Ovenproof: Not surprisingly, a dish or pan that can go in the oven. Pyrex is fine. Watch out for handles on any of your pans, Bakelite handles are not ovenproof. This is not the same as 'flameproof'.

Roll: Dust the work surface with flour to stop it sticking and roll the pastry or dough firmly but evenly with a rolling pin (or clean milk or wine bottle), always rolling away from you. Give the dough a quarter turn and repeat.

TIP: Don't roll from side to side as it stretches the dough, which will then shrink when you cook it.

Slice into rings: To slice an onion into rings, don't bother to peel it, just cut it across in slices the thickness you want, then remove the outer two layers and separate the rest into rings. Discard the ends.

Separate an egg: The easiest way is to break the egg on to a saucer. Then hold an egg cup over the yolk and strain the white into a separate container.

Whip/whisk: Use a balloon whisk to beat the mixture in a circular motion, making sure you lift the mixture up with the whisk as you go to incorporate as much air as possible.

Keeping it clean

This is all pretty much common sense but if you – or any of your housemates – are not strong in that suit, it's worth reminding yourselves of some basic kitchen hygiene to avoid any unpleasant side effects!

In the kitchen

- Wash your hands before you start cooking – you know where they've been

- Clean the work surface before you cook – how clean were your mate's jeans when he sat on it last night?

- Wipe up spills as they happen – and before they go hard and crusty

- Use a clean cloth – otherwise you'll wipe more germs around

- Wash up sooner rather than later – the longer you leave it, the harder it'll be

- Wash up in hot, soapy water (if you wear much-maligned Marigolds, you can put your hands in hot water) – it's much easier!

- Leave to drain rather than dry up with a grubby tea towel – enough said

- Sweep up – food bits on the floor attract mice … and other nasties

- Empty rubbish as soon as the bin is full – if it spills on the floor or the bag splits, that's more clearing up … or mice

Storing food

- Keep an eye on the use-by date and use it up

- If you buy things cheaply on their sell-by date – a good way to save – use it by the use-by date or freeze it immediately

- Don't refreeze anything unless you cook it first – check the labels to make sure chilled food has not been previously frozen. Fish bought in chill cabinets has often already been frozen so if you, or anyone else in your house, eats it, check before you freeze it yourself

- Thaw frozen foods thoroughly – overnight in the fridge is best – and use straight away

- Wrap perishables and keep them in the fridge

- Don't put cans in the fridge – tip half-used canned food into a container with a lid

- Don't leave cooked food lying around – it's a perfect breeding ground for bacteria, not to mention a feeding ground for mice

- Cool leftovers quickly by transferring them from their hot container into a clean cold one. Cover loosely and as soon as they're properly cold, cover and put in the fridge

- If you eat fish, wrap raw fish well and keep it on the bottom shelf in the fridge where it can't drip on anything. Don't put raw and cooked fish on the same shelf

- Don't keep food festering in the fridge – taste and smell are often a good guide to the state of your food: anything that looks, smells or tastes off *is* off!

When you are cooking

- Check instructions on prepared frozen foods to see if they should be cooked from frozen or thawed first

- Try to resist licking your fingers then continuing to cook

- Don't taste and stir with the same spoon. Get out a clean spoon if you want to taste something, and wash it before you taste again

- Check any food is thoroughly cooked through before serving

- Make sure reheated food is piping hot right through – eat it lukewarm and you're asking for trouble

- Never reheat foods more than once

Recipe notes

- I've used an average-sized mug to measure ingredients – or if you get some cup measures from a kitchen shop, use them. The mug should be only loosely filled to the level you would use if making a drink– not crammed full. See the chart for approximate metric equivalents in case you want to measure using scales.

  1 mug = 250 ml liquid

  = 100 g shelled or diced fresh or frozen veg, such as peas

  = 100 g flour and bulgar (cracked wheat)

  = 175 g couscous and lentils

  = 225 g sugar, rice, butter or margarine

- All eggs are medium unless otherwise stated

- All spoon measures are level: 1 tsp = about 5 ml, 1 tbsp = about 15 ml

- All can sizes are approximate – they differ slightly from brand to brand but not by enough to make a difference

- Wash and peel, if necessary, all fresh produce before using

- All preparation and cooking times are approximate

- Always preheat the oven and cook on the centre shelf unless otherwise stated (not so important if you have a fan oven)

- Some recipes serve at least two people, so if you're eating alone have it on two days. You can, in most cases, halve the quantities if you like, but it's just as quick to cook enough for two meals in one go!

- The recipes use dairy products. If you're vegan, omit these and use alternatives, such as soya milk products. Make sure any cheese you use is suitable for vegetarians, too. Labels are usually clearly marked

- Worcestershire sauce is a great flavour booster, but the traditional varieties include anchovies so buy a vegetarian brand from a health food shop

Snacks & light meals

You can always try a Marmite, or other yeast extract, and lettuce sandwich when you're peckish or good old beans on toast but it gets a bit boring after a while. Here's a range of tasty snacks that are very nutritious too and can just as easily be turned into main meals with extra salad, bread or potatoes as appropriate (especially when you're trying to eke out the last few quid of the term).

TIP: If money is getting seriously low, remember that a bowl of wholegrain breakfast cereal with sliced banana or raisins and milk is a very nutritious meal and doesn't have to be just for breakfast.

Stuffed jacket potatoes

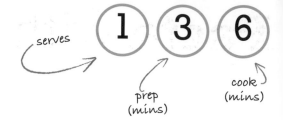

serves → 1   prep (mins) 3   cook (mins) 6

Here are some ideas to spice up that great standby the jacket potato. If you are not cooking anything else in the oven, cook it by the microwave method, then flash it under the grill to crisp the skin. The cooking time is based on that.

1 jacket <u>potato</u> – as big as you like – and as much filling as you want!

1 Cook the potato as described on page 16.

2 Split the potato in half. Mash in a little butter or margarine, then top with any of these:

- Sweetcorn and grated cheese

- Baked beans and grated cheese and a splash of brown sauce

- Chopped cucumber, nuts and mayonnaise

- Chopped tomato and grated cheese

- Marmite, or other yeast extract, and grated cheese

- Hard-boiled egg and mayonnaise

- Cottage cheese and chives

- Pineapple, peanut butter, chopped cucumber and mayonnaise

Pasta with ...

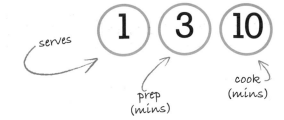

serves 1

prep (mins) 3

cook (mins) 10

Pasta is bound to turn up pretty often in your cooking. The purists would disagree, but in a student kitchen, you can use any pasta for any dish. Generally, a thicker sauce complements a chunkier pasta.

About 2 good handfuls of <u>pasta</u> per person, plus your sauce

1 Cook the pasta as described on page 18.

2 Drain the cooked pasta, then return it to the pan and stir in any of these until piping hot:

• Knob of butter or margarine and lots of grated cheese

• Can of chopped tomatoes with a few dried herbs and grated cheese

• Drained can of peas, a knob of butter or margarine and a little grated cheese

• Egg beaten with a little milk, salt and pepper, a few mixed herbs and/or garlic

• Egg, beaten with a little milk, seasoning and a can of sweetcorn

• Knob of butter or margarine, Marmite, or other yeast extract, and grated cheese

• Peanut butter, a little milk and a pinch of chilli powder – cheese, too, if liked.

Easy rice meals

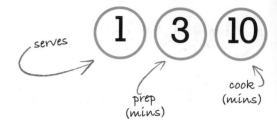

serves 1 3 10

prep (mins)

cook (mins)

Here are some ideas to spice up plain boiled rice to make a tasty and nourishing meal. It's another good thing to have in your cupboard. Different types will take different times to cook so glance at the packet directions before you start.

2 good handfuls of <u>rice</u> per person, plus your flavourings

1 Cook the rice as described on pages 17–18.

2 Drain the cooked rice, then return it to the pan and stir in any of the following until hot:

- Drained can of red kidney beans, some chilli powder and grated cheese

- Drained can of peas, a beaten egg and some soy or veggie Worcestershire sauce

- Can of chopped tomatoes, some dried herbs and grated cheese

- Drained can of pineapple, chick peas and mayonnaise or soy sauce (good hot or cold)

Quick sandwiches

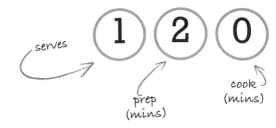

serves **1**

prep (mins) **2**

cook (mins) **0**

Sandwiches are always useful but here are a few interesting ones which will bump up your vitamin C level at the same time as tasting good and being a bit more interesting than ham or cheese.

A few slices of your favourite bread, plus your filling

- **Peanut butter and orange:** Spread 1 slice of bread with peanut butter. Cover with thin slices of peeled orange (cut across the segments). Season with a little pepper and top with a second slice of bread, thinly spread with butter or margarine.

- **Soft cheese and orange:** Prepare as above but use low-fat soft cheese instead of the peanut butter, spread on both slices of bread.

- **Pizza-style:** Lightly spread 2 slices of bread with butter or margarine. Cover 1 slice with grated Mozzarella or Cheddar cheese, top with slices of tomato and a sprinkling of dried basil, then add the second slice of bread.

- **Breakfast salad:** Lightly spread 2 slices of bread with butter or margarine. Spread cottage cheese with pineapple over 1 slice. Spread a little orange marmalade over the other and sandwich together.

- **Banana bite:** Lightly spread 2 slices of bread with low-fat soft cheese. Mash a banana and spread over 1 slice. Top with a segmented satsuma or clementine and then add the other slice of bread.

- **Thai-style:** Spread 2 slices of bread with peanut butter. Sprinkle one with chilli powder and top with some fresh bean sprouts and a drained, chopped ring of canned pineapple. (Add the rest of the pineapple to any of the stir-fries in this book or eat for dessert.) Sprinkle lightly with soy sauce and sandwich together with a second slice of bread lightly spread with butter or margarine.

French toast

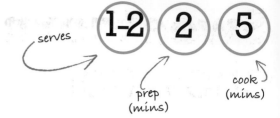

serves 1-2
prep (mins) 2
cook (mins) 5

Add a kick with a pinch of chilli or curry powder with the salt and pepper or, for a sweet option, omit the pepper and salt and toss the cooked bread in a little caster sugar, flavoured with a pinch of ground cinnamon.

2 eggs
1 tbsp milk
Salt and pepper
4 slices of bread
Oil for frying

1 Beat the eggs and milk together in a shallow dish with a little salt and pepper.

2 Cut the slices of bread in half and dip in the egg and milk until completely soaked.

3 Heat a little oil in a frying pan and fry the bread on each side until golden brown.

4 Sprinkle with a little salt and serve straight away.

Sweetcorn chowder

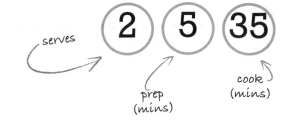

serves **2**

prep (mins) **5**

cook (mins) **35**

This is a good place to suggest it's worth keeping a bag of frozen chopped onion in the freezer (if you have one) as you can then just take out a handful any time you need some without the bother of peeling and chopping.

1 onion, chopped
1 large potato, thinly sliced
200 g/1 small can sweetcorn
1½ mugs boiling water
1 vegetable stock cube
Salt and pepper
¼ mug milk

1 Put all the ingredients except the milk in a saucepan. Bring to the boil, reduce the heat, part-cover and simmer for 30 minutes or until the potatoes are really soft.

2 Stir well with a whisk so the potatoes 'fall' into the liquid and thicken it. Stir in the milk.

3 Taste and re-season if necessary. Heat through and serve.

Thick mixed vegetable soup

serves (1) prep (mins) (2) cook (mins) (2)

You can make this even if you only have a kettle. It's a cheat, of course, but actually tastes really good. Plus adding the canned vegetables does add some nutritional value to the mix.

1 Put the vegetables in a bowl, sprinkle with the soup powder, then gradually stir in the boiling water until thoroughly blended.

2 Leave to stand for 1 minute, then stir, sprinkle with the Parmesan, and enjoy.

225 g/1 small can diced mixed vegetables, drained
1 sachet instant golden vegetable soup
1 mug boiling water
1 tsp grated Parmesan cheese

Mozzarella tomato soup

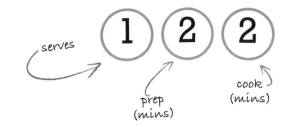

serves **1** prep (mins) **2** cook (mins) **2**

Another instant option for when time and inclination are in short supply. Mozzarella isn't cheap, but you need to buy it fresh so you often find it marked down when near its sell-by date. Buy it then and use it in the next day or so.

1 Mix the cheese, tomato and basil in a bowl, then sprinkle with the soup powder.

2 Pour over the boiling water, stirring all the time, and keep stirring until everything is well blended and the cheese has melted.

½ small round Mozzarella cheese, finely diced
1 tomato, finely chopped
Pinch of dried basil
1 sachet instant tomato soup
1 mug boiling water

Naan wraps

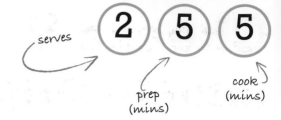

serves **2**
prep (mins) **5**
cook (mins) **5**

Canned pease pudding is just cooked split peas – very nutritious and cheap into the bargain! You could use canned red kidney beans, drained and mashed, instead if you like. It would serve four for a light bite.

2 naan breads
225 g/1 small can pease pudding
2 tsp curry paste or powder
2 tbsp mango chutney or sweet pickle
Lemon juice (optional)
Thinly sliced cucumber
Finely chopped onion

1 Grill the naans as directed on the packet.

2 Meanwhile, heat the pease pudding in a saucepan and stir in the curry paste or powder and chutney or pickle.

3 Spread over the breads, sprinkle with a little lemon juice (if using), then top with slices of cucumber and some finely chopped onion. Fold in half, cut each into 4 wedges and hold in a piece of kitchen paper to eat.

Cheese & tomato **bagel**

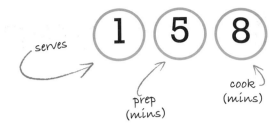

serves (1)

prep (mins) (5)

cook (mins) (8)

Bagels keep really well in the fridge and are great topped with a variety of things but a simple pizza topping is always popular. If they go a bit hard, just use them toasted.

1 Cut the bagel in half and toast under a hot grill.

2 Spread thinly with butter or margarine, then the tomato purée. Top with some sliced tomato then grated cheese and sprinkle with the herbs.

3 Grill until the cheese melts and bubbles.

1 bagel
Butter or margarine for spreading
A little tomato purée
1 tomato, sliced
Handful of Cheddar cheese, grated
Good pinch of dried mixed herbs or basil

Mushroom croissants

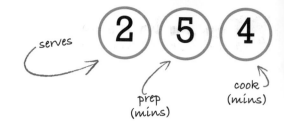

serves **2**

prep (mins) **5**

cook (mins) **4**

Creamed mushrooms are a great standby on toast as well as in croissants or thin with a little milk for a sauce to spoon into jacket-baked potatoes or to toss with pasta shapes.

1 Split the croissants through the middle but not completely, to form a pocket in each.

2 Spread the creamed mushrooms inside.

3 Place under a moderate grill, not too near the heat source, for about 2 minutes on each side until piping hot through. Take care not to let the croissants burn.

2 large or 4 small <u>croissants</u>

215 g/1 small can <u>creamed</u> <u>mushrooms</u>

Nachos

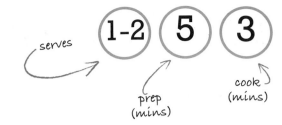

serves **1-2**
prep (mins) **5**
cook (mins) **3**

The rest of the salsa will keep in the fridge. Look out for economy corn tortilla chips in supermarkets – they're fine for this, though some may be broken. Use all but the smallest pieces, then crush the bits and sprinkle over before serving.

1 small bag plain corn tortilla chips
1 jar mild tomato salsa dip
Large handful of grated Cheddar cheese

1 Preheat the grill. Arrange the chips in a shallow flameproof dish or on a plate.

2 Put a teaspoon of salsa on each one.

3 Cover with grated cheese and grill until the cheese has melted. Serve straight away and eat with your fingers.

Spicy potato cakes

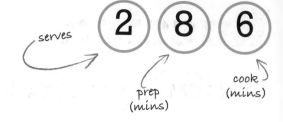

serves 2
prep (mins) 8
cook (mins) 6

These make a tasty lunch or supper dish on their own or topped with fried eggs. You can use curry powder instead of the garam masala and chilli powder if that's what's in the cupboard – or just make them plain without the spices.

2 large potatoes, grated (no need to peel)
1 small onion, grated
½ tsp garam masala
¼ tsp chilli powder
1 egg, beaten
1 tsp plain flour
Salt and pepper
A little oil
SERVE WITH
Mango chutney or other pickle
and salad

1 Mix together the potatoes, onion, spices, egg and flour.

2 Heat enough oil just to cover base of frying pan, then add spoonfuls of the mixture to make little cakes, pressing down well. Fry for 2–3 minutes until golden brown underneath.

3 Turn them over and fry for a further 2–3 minutes until the other side is browned and the cakes are cooked through.

4 Serve hot with mango chutney or other pickle and salad.

Russian
salad pittas

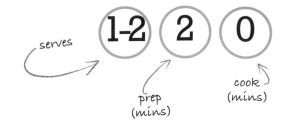

serves 1-2

prep (mins) 2

cook (mins) 0

Canned mixed vegetables are much maligned but are very popular in Spain, mixed with mayonnaise as a tapas. They're really good as a filling for pittas or use to fill flour tortilla wraps.

2 pitta breads
275 g/1 medium can diced mixed vegetables, drained
2 tbsp mayonnaise
Salt and pepper
Shredded lettuce

1 Split the pitta breads along one side and open up to form pockets.

2 Mix the vegetables with the mayonnaise and a little salt and pepper.

3 Spoon into the pitta breads and add a little shredded lettuce.

Hot egg & mayo pitta

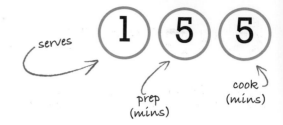

serves **1**

prep (mins) **5**

cook (mins) **5**

This is a cross between scrambled eggs and an omelette. Cook a few sliced mushrooms when you melt the butter before adding the egg for extra flavour and texture.

1 egg

1 tbsp milk

Large pinch of dried mixed herbs

Salt and pepper

Knob of butter or margarine

1 or 2 pitta breads

Shredded lettuce

Mayonnaise

1 Beat the egg with the milk, herbs and a little salt and pepper.

2 Heat the butter or margarine in a small frying pan and fry the egg, stirring all the time until scrambled, then cook for 1 minute more to brown the base.

3 Split the pitta bread along one side and open out to form a pocket. Fill with the egg mixture and add some lettuce and mayonnaise. Eat straight away.

Hummus & sesame **wraps**

serves **2** prep (mins) **2** cook (mins) **2**

Hummus is very nutritious and a great option for a vegetarian snack. Here I've use it as a wrap filler but it's great as a dip just with warm pittas and some raw vegetable 'dippers'.

1 Spread the hummus thickly on the tortillas.

2 Sprinkle with a few sesame seeds

3 Scatter the olives over, if using, add some lettuce and pepper slices. Add a squeeze of lemon juice, if using, fold in the sides then roll up.

1 small tub <u>hummus</u>
1–2 flour <u>tortillas</u>
1–2 tsp <u>sesame seeds</u>
A few chopped <u>stoned olives</u>
(optional)
Shredded <u>lettuce</u>
½–1 sliced <u>green</u> or <u>red pepper</u>
Squeeze of <u>lemon juice</u>
(optional)

Quesadillas

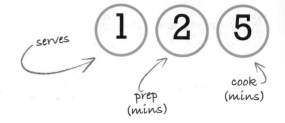

serves

prep (mins)

cook (mins)

These are good with a little tomato salsa spread evenly on one tortilla before topping with the cheese. Keep the rest of the tortillas wrapped in the fridge or freeze for another day.

2 flour tortillas
Handful of grated Cheddar cheese
SERVE WITH
Salad

1 Heat a non-stick frying pan, big enough to take the flour tortilla flat. When it feels hot when you hold your hand about 5 cm above the surface, turn the heat to moderate and add one of the tortillas.

2 Quickly spread the cheese over and top with the second tortilla. Press it down firmly with a fish slice. Fry until the cheese is melting and the base is browning slightly, pressing down all the time.

3 Carefully flip the whole thing over guiding the top with your hand (or invert it on to a plate and slide back in). Fry the other side until cheese has completely melted.

4 Slide on to a plate and cut in wedges. Serve with salad bits.

French
cheese loaf

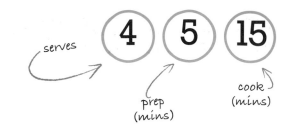

serves **4** — prep (mins) **5** — cook (mins) **15**

You can cook this under a moderate grill for about 15 minutes, turning occasionally, then open up the foil to brown the top but take care not to let it burn.

1 French stick
Butter or margarine for spreading
1 round Camembert, thinly sliced
3 tomatoes, sliced
Dried mixed herbs

1 Preheat the oven to 220°C/425°F/gas 7/fan oven 200°C.

2 Cut the French stick into slices but not right through the base.

3 Spread with a little butter or margarine between each slice.

4 Add a slice of Camembert and tomato, sprinkled with herbs, between each slice.

5 Wrap completely in foil and bake in the oven for 15 minutes or until the crust feels crispy and the cheese has melted.

Chilli corn & banana wedges

serves **2**

prep (mins) **5**

cook (mins) **10**

These are good served with some shredded lettuce or cucumber slices packed in with the eggy wedges. If you like lots of spice, try adding some pickled jalapeño slices from a jar.

1 small unripe banana, thickly sliced
Butter or margarine for frying
A good pinch of dried chilli flakes or powder
2 eggs
1 tbsp water
200 g/1 small can sweetcorn
Salt and pepper
Knob of butter or margarine
SERVE WITH
4–6 crispy tacos or 2–3 split warm pitta breads

1 Melt a large knob of butter or margarine in a frying pan, add the banana slices, sprinkle with the chilli and fry for 1 minute, turning once. Remove from the pan.

2 Beat the eggs with the water and stir in the can of sweetcorn. Season to taste.

3 Melt a knob of butter or margarine in the frying pan and pour in the egg and corn mixture. Fry, lifting and stirring, until set and golden brown underneath.

4 Scatter the banana slices over and put the frying pan under a hot grill briefly to brown the top.

5 Cut in wedges, place in crispy tacos or warm pitta bread pockets.

Fish finger rolls

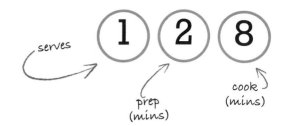

serves 1
prep (mins) 2
cook (mins) 8

If you eat fish, this is quick and tasty. You can use breaded fish instead of the fingers, but it'll be more expensive and will take longer to cook. Beware of economy fish fingers, they're made of minced dubious bits of fish!

4 <u>fish fingers</u>
1 soft <u>bread roll</u>
1 slice of <u>cheese</u>
Ready-made <u>tartare sauce</u> or <u>mayonnaise</u>
<u>Lettuce</u>, shredded

1 Cook the fish fingers according to the packet directions.

2 Split the roll and lay the fish fingers on the bottom half.

3 Top with a slice of cheese and flash under a hot grill to melt the cheese.

4 Top with some tartare sauce or mayonnaise, shredded lettuce and then the lid of the roll.

Tzaziki with pittas

serves **1-2** prep (mins) **5** cook (mins) **0**

You can make your own version of this classic Greek dip in minutes – and cheaper than buying it ready made. Use anything you have to dip in – pittas, sticks of vegetables, crackers or crisps. Thick yoghurt works best.

1 Squeeze the grated cucumber to remove excess moisture.

2 Mix together everything except the pittas. If you have time, leave in the fridge for a few hours.

3 Cut the pittas into strips and serve with the dip.

5 cm piece of <u>cucumber</u>, grated
5 tbsp <u>Greek-style plain yoghurt</u>
1 tsp <u>olive oil</u>
½ tsp <u>garlic purée</u>
1 tsp dried <u>mint</u>
<u>Salt and pepper</u>
<u>Pitta breads</u>

Pitta pockets

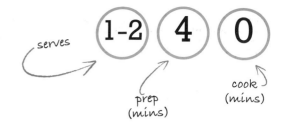

serves 1-2   4   0

prep (mins)

cook (mins)

It's worth bothering to warm the breads first – as in step 1. If they are cold, they'll often split, stick together, crumble or tear, which is really annoying if you want to fill them, and it's very messy when you come to eat them.

1 Toast or microwave the pittas just to heat through enough to puff up. Split along one long edge to form a pocket.

2 Add the shredded lettuce, tomato, cucumber and one of the suggested fillings.

3 Finish with the mayonnaise.

2 pitta breads
Handful of lettuce, shredded
1 tomato, sliced
A few slices of cucumber
FOR THE FILLING CHOOSE
FROM
Chopped hard boiled egg, feta cubes, mashed canned pulses
Or tuna or mashed pilchards, if you eat fish
1 tbsp mayonnaise

Vegetable-based dishes

Nothing is etched in stone, so ring the changes with different vegetables that take your fancy (or are particularly cheap at the time). As a rough guide, you can substitute any root vegetable for another, any green vegetable for another and so on. Make sure you cut them up to a similar size so they cook in roughly the same time. Many of the recipes serve two or three people – enough for two days for one person. Double the quantities if you're cooking for flatmates or friends.

Minestra

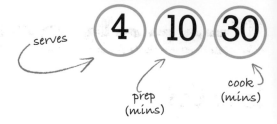

serves **4** prep (mins) **10** cook (mins) **30**

Grating the vegetables makes sure they cook evenly but you could chop them fairly finely if you prefer, just simmer the soup for a little longer to make sure they are soft.

1 Empty the tomatoes into a large pan and break up with a wooden spoon.

2 Add the remaining ingredients. Bring to the boil, reduce the heat, part-cover and simmer for 20 minutes until all the vegetables are really tender. Taste and re-season if necessary.

3 Serve sprinkled with grated cheese.

400 g/1 large can <u>tomatoes</u>
1 <u>onion</u>, grated
1 large <u>carrot</u>, grated
1 large <u>potato</u>, grated
¼ small <u>cabbage</u>, shredded
3 mugs <u>boiling water</u>
1 <u>vegetable stock cube</u>
425 g/1 large can <u>haricot beans</u>, drained
Small handful of <u>macaroni</u> or <u>crushed spaghetti</u>
½ tsp <u>dried mixed herbs</u> or <u>oregano</u>
<u>Salt and pepper</u>
SERVE WITH
<u>Grated Cheddar</u> or <u>Parmesan-style cheese</u>, suitable for vegetarians

French onion soup

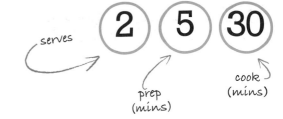

serves **2**

prep (mins) **5**

cook (mins) **30**

You can cheat and use a can of fried onion instead of all the frying – a very useful thing to have in the cupboard. Drain them well before you use them, though, as they tend to be a bit oily and contine from step 2.

2 tbsp <u>butter</u> or <u>margarine</u>
2 large <u>onions</u>, roughly chopped
2 tsp <u>light brown sugar</u>
2 mugs <u>boiling water</u>
1 <u>vegetable stock cube</u>
<u>Salt and pepper</u>
2 slices of <u>French bread</u>
Large handful of <u>Cheddar</u> or <u>Gruyère cheese</u>, grated

1 Melt the butter or margarine in a saucepan and fry the onions for 5 minutes, stirring, until turning golden.

2 Add the sugar and continue frying for 3–4 minutes until a rich golden brown, stirring all the time.

3 Stir in the boiling water, crumbled stock cube and a little salt and pepper, bring to the boil, reduce the heat, part-cover and simmer gently for 15–20 minutes until the onions are really soft. Taste and re-season if necessary.

4 When ready to serve, toast the bread on both sides. Top with the cheese and grill until melted. Ladle the soup into bowls and float the toasted cheese on top.

Hearty
vegetable soup

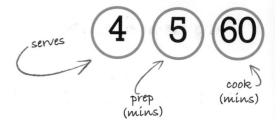

serves → **4**

prep (mins) → **5**

cook (mins) → **60**

You may as well use all the vegetables, then store the cooked soup in the fridge and heat it up over the next couple of days if there's not so many of you. Serve with plenty of crusty bread.

1 Put all the ingredients in a large saucepan. Bring to the boil, reduce the heat, part-cover and simmer very gently for 1 hour until the vegetables are really tender.

2 Taste and re-season if necessary.

3 Ladle into bowls or mugs and add a few cubes of cheese, if liked.

1 large <u>potato</u>, cut into small dice

1 small <u>cauliflower</u>, cut into small florets

1 small <u>swede</u>, cut into small dice

1 <u>carrot</u>, cut into small dice

1 <u>onion</u>, chopped

4½ mugs <u>boiling water</u>

2 <u>vegetable stock cubes</u>

<u>Salt and pepper</u>

1 tbsp <u>tomato purée</u>

1 tsp dried <u>mixed herbs</u>

SERVE WITH

A few small cubes of <u>melting cheese</u> (like Cheddar, Edam, Camembert or Gruyère)

Curried
parsnip soup

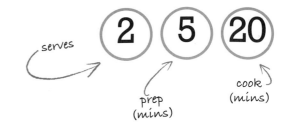

serves **2**

prep (mins) **5**

cook (mins) **20**

You can substitute carrots instead for the parsnips if you prefer. If you've got any leftover cooked rice, throw it in before reheating at the end for an even more filling meal.

1 large _parsnip_, sliced

1 large _potato_, sliced

1 _onion_, chopped

2 mugs _boiling water_

1 _vegetable stock cube_

½ tsp _curry powder_ or _paste_

Salt and pepper

A little _milk_

SERVE WITH

Naan bread

1 Put all the ingredients except the milk in a saucepan. Bring to the boil, reduce the heat, part-cover and simmer for about 15 minutes or until the vegetables are really soft.

2 Strain off the stock into a bowl. Mash the vegetables well, then stir in the stock again. Thin with a little milk if liked.

3 Taste and re-season if necessary.

4 Reheat and serve with naan bread.

Peanut soup

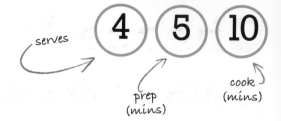

serves **4** **5** **10**

prep (mins)

cook (mins)

This is so easy, you might as well make enough for a couple of days. You can spice it with a pinch of chilli powder in the flour or add a few drops of Tabasco at the end. It's also good with toasted cheese on top, as for French Onion Soup.

1 small <u>onion</u>, grated

1 <u>carrot</u>, grated

Large knob of <u>butter</u> or <u>margarine</u>

3 tbsp <u>plain flour</u>

4 mugs <u>boiling water</u>

2 chicken or vegetable <u>stock cubes</u>

½ jar <u>smooth peanut butter</u>

1 mug <u>single cream</u> or <u>milk</u>

<u>Salt and pepper</u>

SERVE WITH

<u>Crusty bread</u>

1 Fry the onion and carrot in the butter or margarine in a large pan for 2 minutes, stirring.

2 Sprinkle in the flour and cook, stirring, for 1 minute. Remove from the heat.

3 Gradually blend in the boiling water and add the stock cubes. Return to the heat, bring to the boil, stirring, turn down the heat and cook gently for 5 minutes.

4 Blend in the peanut butter and cream or milk, using a whisk or wooden spoon. Reheat, stirring all the time, but do not boil. Taste and season, if necessary.

5 Serve with lots of crusty bread.

Cheese & potato bake

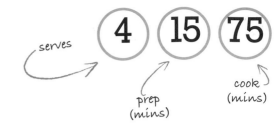

serves **4**   prep (mins) **15**   cook (mins) **75**

It's worth making enough for 4 people. The rest will keep in the fridge and is delicious eaten cold with pickles. You can, of course, use Cheddar or Edam instead of Swiss cheese.

3–4 large <u>potatoes</u>, thinly sliced
Knob of <u>butter</u> or <u>margarine</u>
1½ mugs grated <u>Gruyère</u> or <u>Emmental cheese</u>
<u>Salt and pepper</u>
2 <u>eggs</u>
150 ml/1 small carton <u>single cream</u>
½ mug <u>milk</u>
1 tsp <u>garlic</u> from a jar or tube
SERVE WITH
<u>Salad</u>

1 Put the sliced potatoes in a saucepan of cold water. Bring to the boil and cook for 2 minutes. Drain in a colander, then rinse with cold water to cool them quickly.

2 Preheat the oven to 180°C/350°F/gas 4/fan oven 160°C.

3 Use the butter or margarine to grease an ovenproof serving dish, big enough to take about 5 mugfuls of water.

4 Put a layer of potato slices in the base. Cover with a little of the cheese and a little salt and pepper. Repeat the layers until all the potatoes and cheese are used, finishing with a layer of cheese.

5 Whisk the eggs, cream and milk together with the garlic in a small bowl and pour over the potatoes.

6 Bake in the oven for 1–1¼ hours until the potatoes are tender and the top is golden brown.

7 Serve hot with salad.

Mediterranean veg with **eggs**

serves **2** prep (mins) **10** cook (mins) **25**

If you prefer it hot, add ¼ tsp chilli powder and add dried oregano instead of the basil. If eating alone, spoon out half the mixture before adding 2 eggs. Heat the rest the next day, add 2 more eggs and cook as step 3.

1 Heat the oil in a large frying pan. Add the vegetables and fry for 5 minutes, stirring until softened.

2 Add the beans, water, stock cube and tomato purée or ketchup. Season lightly. Stir well, turn down the heat, cover and simmer very gently for about 10 minutes until really soft, stirring once or twice.

3 Make 4 'wells' in the mixture. Break an egg into each. Cover again and cook gently for 5–10 minutes until cooked to your liking. Serve straight from the pan with crusty bread and a salad.

2 tbsp <u>olive</u> or <u>sunflower oil</u>
1 <u>onion</u>, chopped
1 small <u>aubergine</u>, diced
1 <u>green</u> or <u>red pepper</u>, diced
425 g/1 large can <u>black eyed beans</u>, drained
½ mug <u>boiling water</u>
½ <u>vegetable stock cube</u>
2 tbsp <u>tomato purée</u> or <u>ketchup</u>
¼ tsp <u>dried basil</u>
<u>Salt and pepper</u>
4 <u>eggs</u>
SERVE WITH
<u>Crusty bread</u> and <u>salad</u>

Grilled glazed root satay

serves 2-3 | prep (mins) 15 | cook (mins) 20

This is a favourite of mine for a main meal or as party food (thread on cocktail sticks and serve with the sauce as a dip, omitting the rice). Vary the vegetables according to what's available. You could just use baby potatoes and carrots.

2 large carrots, cut into bite-sized chunks

1 small swede, cut into bite-sized chunks

Knob of butter or margarine

1 tbsp clear honey

FOR THE SAUCE

5 tbsp peanut butter

⅔ mug milk

¼ tsp chilli powder

Salt and pepper

SERVE WITH

Boiled rice

1 Cook the vegetables in boiling, lightly salted water until just tender. Drain, rinse with cold water and drain again.

2 Thread alternately on kebab skewers. Lay on foil on a grill rack.

3 Melt the butter or margarine and honey together and brush over the kebabs. Grill, turning occasionally, for about 20 minutes until lightly golden, brushing with the butter or margarine and honey mixture.

4 Meanwhile, put the sauce ingredients in a saucepan and heat through, stirring.

5 Serve the kebabs on a bed of boiled rice with the sauce spooned over.

Ratatouille
supper

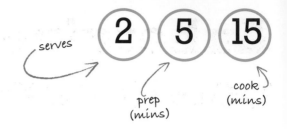

serves **2**   prep (mins) **5**   cook (mins) **15**

Make this go further if there's more of you – or be more substantial – by adding a drained can of cannellini beans or brown lentils to the ratatouille before heating it up.

2–3 large <u>potatoes</u>, peeled and cut in small chunks

<u>Salt</u>

Knob of <u>butter</u> or <u>margarine</u>

425 g/1 large can <u>ratatouille</u>

2 large handfuls of grated <u>Cheddar cheese</u>

1   Boil the potatoes in lightly salted water for about 5 minutes until tender. Drain and mash with a fork or potato masher, adding a knob of butter or margarine.

2   Meanwhile preheat the grill.

3   Heat the ratatouille in a saucepan until piping hot.

4   Spoon into 2 individual flameproof dishes. Top with the potato and rough up with a fork. Cover with the grated cheese. Grill until golden and bubbling.

Aubergine & potato **curry**

For a cheaper version, use 2 extra potatoes and omit the aubergine. It's worth making this quantity as it keeps well in the fridge and, if anything, the flavour improves with keeping a day or two.

3 tbsp sunflower oil

1 onion, sliced

1 tsp garlic from a jar or tube

1 large new potato, scrubbed and diced

1 large aubergine, diced

1 tbsp curry paste or powder

½ mug boiling water

½ vegetable stock cube

425 g/1 large can green or brown lentils, drained

2 mugs frozen peas

Salt and pepper

1 small carton plain yoghurt

2 tbsp chopped fresh coriander (optional)

SERVE WITH

Naan breads

1 Heat the oil in a large saucepan. Fry the onion, stirring, for 2 minutes.

2 Add the garlic, potato, aubergine and curry powder or paste and cook, stirring, for 3 minutes.

3 Add the water and stock cube, stir well, cover with a lid, turn down the heat and cook gently for 15 minutes.

4 Stir in the lentils, peas, some salt and pepper and the yoghurt. Continue to cook gently, uncovered, for a further 15 minutes until everything is tender and bathed in sauce.

5 Warm the naan breads briefly under the grill.

6 Stir the coriander, if using, into the curry, taste and add more salt and pepper if necessary.

7 Serve hot with the naan breads.

almost finished

Sweet & sour beans

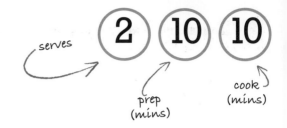

serves **2** — prep (mins) **10** — cook (mins) **10**

Traditional Worcestershire sauce contains anchovies so if you are a true veggie you will need to buy it from a health food shop. You can use topped and tailed French or stringless, flat helda beans, cut in short lengths, instead of runners.

450 g <u>runner beans</u>, stringed and diagonally sliced
2 slabs of <u>Chinese egg noodles</u>
Large knob of <u>butter</u> or <u>margarine</u>
4–6 cup <u>mushrooms</u>, sliced
2 handfuls of <u>raw peanuts</u>
2 tbsp <u>Worcestershire-style sauce</u>
1 tbsp <u>soy sauce</u>
2 tbsp <u>clear honey</u>
2 tbsp <u>vinegar</u> (preferably red wine but any will do)

1 Bring a large pan of water to the boil over a high heat. Add a good pinch of salt, the runner beans and noodles. Bring back to the boil, then cook for 5 minutes until just tender. Drain.

2 Melt the butter or margarine in the bean saucepan. Add the mushrooms and cook, stirring, for 2 minutes.

3 Add the nuts, Worcestershire sauce, soy sauce, honey and vinegar and stir well.

4 Return the runner beans and noodles to the pan. Cook over a low heat, lifting and stirring gently, until piping hot. Serve in warm bowls.

Mushroom
stroganoff

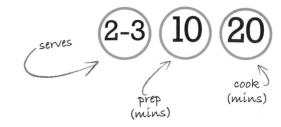

serves **2-3** **10** **20**

prep (mins)

cook (mins)

This has a delicious rich mushroom flavour. It will serve up to 4 people if you add more pasta or rice to accompany it! It's also good with some cooked green beans added at the end of step 2.

3 tbsp <u>butter</u> or <u>margarine</u>
1 small <u>onion</u>, chopped
1 tsp <u>garlic</u> from a jar or tube
450 g <u>mushrooms</u>, quartered
5 tbsp <u>white wine</u> or <u>cider</u>
1½ tsp <u>cornflour</u>
1 small carton <u>soured cream</u>, <u>crème fraîche</u> or <u>plain yoghurt</u>
<u>Salt and pepper</u>
A little chopped <u>fresh parsley</u> or a few <u>dried chives</u> (optional)
SERVE WITH
<u>Plain boiled rice</u> or <u>tagliatelle</u>

1 Melt the butter or margarine in a large pan and fry the onion and garlic for 2 minutes, stirring.

2 Add the mushrooms, cover and cook gently for 10 minutes. Remove the lid and continue cooking until all the liquid has evaporated, stirring occasionally.

3 Add the wine or cider and simmer for 5 minutes.

4 Blend the cornflour with a little water and stir into the pan with the cream or yoghurt. Simmer, stirring, for 4 minutes until thickened.

5 Season to taste and serve sprinkled with parsley or chives, if liked, on a bed of rice or pasta.

Vegetable
risotto

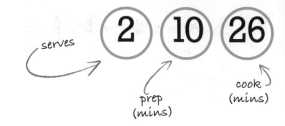

serves **2**

prep (mins) **10**

cook (mins) **26**

You can ring the changes with any vegetables of your choice – look out for what's in season – just make sure you cut root vegetables up fairly small or they won't cook in the time.

3 tbsp <u>sunflower</u> or <u>olive oil</u>

1 <u>onion</u>, chopped

1 <u>carrot</u>, finely diced or thinly sliced

1 <u>red pepper</u>, diced

1 <u>courgette</u>, diced or sliced

2 <u>tomatoes</u>, chopped

½ mug <u>long-grain rice</u>

1¼ mugs <u>boiling water</u>

1 <u>vegetable stock cube</u>

½ tsp <u>dried basil</u>

<u>Salt and pepper</u>

1 tbsp chopped <u>fresh parsley</u> (optional)

2 handfuls of <u>grated Cheddar</u>, <u>Mozzarella</u> or <u>Parmesan-style cheese</u>, suitable for vegetarians

1 Heat the oil in a large saucepan and fry all the prepared vegetables, stirring over a moderate heat for 5 minutes.

2 Add the rice and stir for 1 minute.

3 Add the remaining ingredients and bring to the boil. Stir well, turn down the heat to very low, then cover and simmer very gently for 20 minutes without stirring. The rice should be just tender and have absorbed nearly all the liquid.

4 Stir well and serve sprinkled with grated cheese.

Vegetable stir-fry

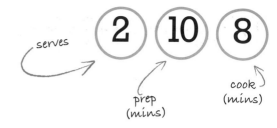

serves 2
prep (mins) 10
cook (mins) 8

You can add a handful of raw peanuts or cashews – very tasty but quite expensive – or a drained can of sweetcorn or broad beans to this recipe for extra protein and extra flavour, if you like.

1 Heat the oil in a wok or large frying pan. Add the vegetables and stir-fry for 4 minutes.

2 Drain the pineapple juice into a bowl, reserving the fruit, then blend the remaining ingredients except the bean sprouts into the juice.

3 Add to the stir-fried vegetables and simmer for 2 minutes, stirring.

4 Add the reserved pineapple and bean sprouts and heat through, stirring for 2 minutes.

5 Serve with boiled rice or Chinese egg noodles.

1 tbsp oil
1 small onion, sliced
1 small pepper, sliced
¼ cucumber, cut into matchsticks
1 carrot, cut into matchsticks
300 g/1 small can pineapple pieces in natural juice
1 tbsp tomato ketchup
1 tbsp soy sauce
1 tbsp vinegar
2 tsp clear honey
1½ tsp cornflour
2 tbsp water
1 small bag fresh bean sprouts or 425 g/1 large can
SERVE WITH
Boiled rice or Chinese egg noodles

Vegetable crusty-top

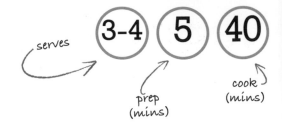
Part-cook some jacket potatoes in the microwave then pop them in the oven to finish cooking with the crumble for a more substantial meal. Or grill the dish once you've topped it with the bread and cheese but take care it doesn't burn.

2 tbsp oil

1 red pepper, sliced

4 courgettes, sliced

8 cup mushrooms, sliced

400 g/1 large can tomatoes

1 tsp garlic from a jar or tube

Salt and pepper

½ tsp dried basil or mixed herbs

1 mug grated Cheddar or Red Leicester cheese

3 slices wholemeal bread, buttered and diced

1 Heat the oil in a flameproof casserole or saucepan and fry the pepper, courgettes and mushrooms for about 3 minutes, stirring, until slightly softened.

2 Add the tomatoes and break up with a wooden spoon. Stir in the remaining ingredients except the cheese and breadcrumbs. Reduce the heat, cover and simmer for 10 minutes, stirring occasionally. Turn into an ovenproof dish if cooked in a saucepan.

3 Preheat the oven to 200°C/400°F/gas 6/fan oven 180°C.

4 Mix together the cheese and cubed bread and sprinkle over the top. Bake in the oven for about 25 minutes until turning golden on top.

Vegetable
dolmas

To use the whole can of ratatouille, you need to make 8, so make it when friends come round or eat some and have the rest cold or reheated over the next couple of days. If you're hungry, you'll probably manage 3 or even 4 rolls.

8 large <u>cabbage leaves</u>

425 g/1 large can <u>ratatouille</u>

2 tbsp <u>long-grain rice</u>

1 mug <u>boiling water</u>

1 <u>vegetable stock cube</u>

1 tbsp <u>tomato purée</u>

<u>Salt and pepper</u>

SERVE WITH

<u>Grated Cheddar cheese</u> and

<u>crusty bread</u>

1   Cut out the thick central base to the stalk of the leaves in a 'v' shape.

2   Bring a pan of water to the boil. Drop in the leaves and blanch for 3 minutes. Drain, rinse with cold water and drain again. Dry on kitchen paper.

3   Mix the ratatouille with the raw rice.

4   Lay a leaf on a board and overlap the two points where the stalk was. Put an eighth of the filling on top. Fold in the sides and roll up.

5   Place in a large saucepan. Repeat with the remaining cabbage and filling, packing the rolls into the pan in a single layer.

6   Mix the boiling water, stock cube and tomato purée together and pour around the cabbage rolls. Season lightly.

7   Bring to the boil, cover, reduce the heat until bubbling very gently round the edges and cook for about 30 minutes or until the cabbage and rice are tender. Spoon on to warm plates and spoon any juices over.

8   Serve hot, sprinkled with grated cheese with lots of crusty bread.

almost finished

Couscous
stuffed peppers

Make all 4 peppers as they'll keep in the fridge for several days, or serve when friends come round. Good with lots of crusty bread. Or you could do this recipe on one day with half a can of ratatouille and make dolmas (page 65) the next.

4 large <u>peppers</u>
425 g/1 large can <u>ratatouille</u>
⅓ mug <u>couscous</u>
½ tsp <u>dried oregano</u>
4 handfuls of grated strong <u>Cheddar</u> or crumbled <u>blue cheese</u>
<u>salt and pepper</u>
2 mugs <u>boiling water</u>
1 <u>vegetable stock cube</u>

1 Cut the tops off the peppers about 8 mm down from the stalk end. Pull out the cores and seeds. Tap the peppers firmly on the work surface, cut-sides down, to remove any loose seeds. Make sure the peppers will stand upright; if not, trim a very thin slice off the bases (take care not to make a hole in the flesh).

2 Mix the ratatouille with the couscous, oregano and half the cheese. Taste and add a little salt and pepper, if necessary.

3 Stand the peppers in a saucepan and spoon the ratatouille mixture into them. Top with the remaining cheese and rest the pepper 'lids' on top. Pour the boiling water around and add the stock cube. Bring to the boil, reduce the heat to low, cover and cook gently for about 45 minutes until the peppers are tender.

4 Transfer the peppers to plates and spoon a little of the cooking stock over, if liked. Alternatively, leave to cool, then chill before serving.

Curried potato nests

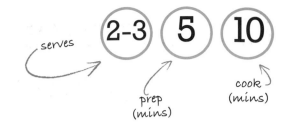

serves 2-3 · prep (mins) 5 · cook (mins) 10

If you have a metal colander, you can put the frozen vegetables in it and put it over the pan of potatoes, cover the vegetables with the saucepan lid and steam them while cooking the potatoes.

3-4 large <u>potatoes</u>, peeled and cut in small chunks

2 tbsp <u>milk</u>

A knob of <u>butter</u> or <u>margarine</u>

1 tsp <u>tomato purée</u>

½ tsp <u>curry powder</u> or <u>paste</u>

225 g/1 small packet <u>frozen mixed vegetables with sweetcorn</u>

2 large handfuls of grated <u>Cheddar cheese</u>

SERVE WITH

<u>Mango chutney</u> or <u>sweet pickle</u>

1 Cook the potatoes in boiling, lightly salted water until tender, about 10 minutes. Drain and mash with the milk, butter or margarine, tomato purée and curry powder or paste.

2 Meanwhile, cook the frozen vegetables according to packet directions. Drain.

3 Spoon the mashed curried potato in a ring on 2 serving plates. Spoon the hot vegetables into the centre and sprinkle with the grated cheese before serving.

Vegetable
cottage pie

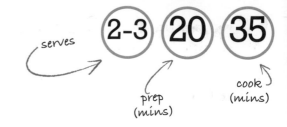

This takes a bit more time to prepare but it isn't difficult and taste good! It's ideal when you're eating with a friend but leftovers can be reheated on a plate or in the microwave.

2–3 large potatoes, cut into smallish chunks

Knob of butter or margarine

1 tbsp milk

¼ x 1 kg packet frozen chunky mixed vegetables

1 slice of wholemeal bread, chopped

400 g/1 large can baked beans

1 tsp Marmite, or other yeast extract

2 tbsp boiling water

½ tsp dried mixed herbs

Salt and pepper

Large handful of grated Cheddar cheese

1 Boil the potatoes in lightly salted water until just tender. Drain and mash with a potato masher or fork. Beat in the butter or margarine and the milk.

2 Preheat the oven to 200°C/400°F/gas 6/ fan oven 180°C.

3 Meanwhile, boil the vegetables in lightly salted water in a separate pan until tender. Drain. Mix the vegetables with the bread and beans in an ovenproof serving dish.

4 Blend the Marmite with the water. Stir into the dish with the herbs until thoroughly mixed. Season to taste.

5 Top with the mashed potato, then sprinkle with the cheese.

6 Bake in the oven for about 35 minutes until golden.

Vegetable curry

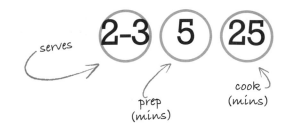

serves **2-3** prep **5** (mins) cook **25** (mins)

Throw in a handful of raisins or sultanas, if you have any, and serve slices of banana or apple as a tasty side dish. To be more substantial, add a can of drained chickpeas – it'll serve up to 4 people then.

2 <u>potatoes</u>, diced

2 <u>carrots</u>, diced

1 small <u>cauliflower</u>, cut into florets

1 tbsp <u>oil</u>

1 <u>onion</u>, chopped

1 tbsp <u>curry powder</u>

1 tbsp <u>tomato purée</u>

½ tsp <u>garlic</u> from a jar or tube

½ mug <u>frozen peas</u>

¼ block of <u>creamed coconut</u>, cut into small pieces

2 tsp <u>lemon juice</u>

<u>Salt and pepper</u>

SERVE WITH

<u>Boiled rice</u>

1 Cook the potatoes, carrots and cauliflower in boiling, salted water for 5 minutes until almost cooked. Drain, reserving the cooking water.

2 Meanwhile, heat the oil in a separate saucepan and fry the onion, stirring, for 2 minutes.

3 Add the remaining ingredients except the salt and pepper. Gradually stir in enough of the reserved cooking water to make a thickish sauce. Stir until the creamed coconut has dissolved, then season to taste.

4 Add the part-cooked vegetables, stir gently, then cover and simmer over a gentle heat, stirring occasionally, until the vegetables are just tender and bathed in a rich sauce. Thin with a little more of the cooking water if necessary.

almost finished

5 Serve on a bed of boiled rice.

Tabbouleh
with corn

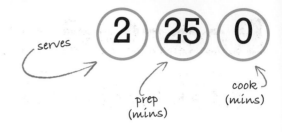

serves 2

prep (mins) 25

cook (mins) 0

Jazz it up with a handful of chopped nuts, pine nuts, pumpkin or sunflower seeds, or a few sliced olives. If you invest in a bag of fresh parsley for this, put the rest in the freezer and use crumbled from frozen when needed.

¾ mug <u>bulgar wheat</u>

<u>Boiling water</u>

½ tsp <u>salt</u>

1½ tbsp <u>sunflower</u> or <u>olive oil</u>

1½ tbsp <u>lemon juice</u> or <u>vinegar</u>

½ tsp <u>garlic</u> from a jar or tube

A large handful of <u>fresh parsley</u>, chopped (it's worth it in this!)

½ tsp <u>dried mint</u>

200 g/1 small can <u>sweetcorn</u>, drained

<u>Pepper</u>

2 <u>tomatoes</u>, chopped

¼ <u>cucumber</u>, chopped

½ <u>small onion</u>, sliced and separated into rings

1 Put the wheat in a bowl and pour over just enough boiling water to cover. Sprinkle with the salt, stir and leave to stand for 15–20 minutes until swollen and the wheat has absorbed all or nearly all the liquid. Drain if necessary.

2 Drizzle over the oil and lemon juice or vinegar, add the garlic, herbs, corn and some pepper. Mix well, leave to cool, then chill, in the fridge.

3 Just before serving, stir in the tomatoes and cucumber and scatter the onion rings over.

Roasted nut tabbouleh

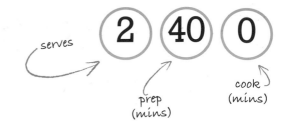

serves 2 — prep (mins) 40 — cook (mins) 0

You really do need fresh herbs for this but use fresh basil instead of coriander if you prefer. The easiest way to chop them is to put the leaves in a cup or mug and snip them with scissors.

¾ mug <u>bulgar wheat</u>
<u>Boiling water</u>
<u>Salt and pepper</u>
2 <u>spring onions</u>, finely chopped
5 cm piece of <u>cucumber</u>, chopped
1 <u>red pepper</u>, chopped
3 tbsp chopped <u>fresh parsley</u>
1 tbsp chopped <u>fresh coriander</u>
2 tbsp <u>olive oil</u>
1 tbsp <u>lemon juice</u>
½ tsp <u>garlic</u> from a jar or tube
Handful of <u>roasted peanuts</u>
Handful of <u>toasted pine nuts</u>

1 Put the bulgar in a large bowl. Add just enough boiling water to cover, stir and leave to stand for 15–20 minutes or until swollen, soft and most or all of the water has been absorbed. Drain, if necessary, and leave to cool.

2 Add the remaining ingredients. Toss well. Season to taste.

3 Cover and chill for at least 2 hours before serving to allow the flavours to develop.

Aubergine & mozzarella grill

serves **2** prep (mins) **10** cook (mins) **5**

This makes a great main meal but if you're out to impress friends, serve it as a starter for 4 before a pasta dish. If eating alone, store the second one covered in the fridge before grilling, then just cook it when you're ready to eat it.

6 tbsp olive oil

1 large aubergine, sliced

Salt and pepper

½ mug passata

½ tsp dried basil

125 g Mozzarella, thinly sliced

2 tbsp grated Parmesan-style cheese, suitable for vegetarians

1 Heat the oil in a frying pan over a high heat. Fry the aubergine slices until golden on both sides. Drain on kitchen paper, then arrange in 2 individual flameproof dishes.

2 Sprinkle with salt and pepper. Spoon the passata over the aubergines and sprinkle with the basil. Top with the Mozzarella, then the Parmesan.

3 Preheat the grill. Remove the grill rack and place the dishes in the grill pan. Grill until the cheese melts and bubbles. Serve straight away.

Spiced corn & raisin salad

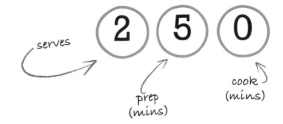

serves **2**

prep (mins) **5**

cook (mins) **0**

This is a great throw-together meal when time is short and you can't be bothered to cook. Any leftovers will keep in the fridge for a couple of days in a covered container. It's good topped with wedges of hard-boiled egg too.

1 Mix all the ingredients except the lettuce and tomatoes in a bowl.

2 Pile on to a bed of shredded lettuce and arrange a few tomato wedges around.

3 Serve with crusty bread.

350 g/1 large can <u>sweetcorn</u>, drained

1 tsp <u>dried chives</u>

1 tbsp <u>mayonnaise</u>

1 tsp <u>lemon juice</u> or <u>vinegar</u>

1 tbsp <u>sweet pickle</u> or <u>mango chutney</u>

A handful of <u>raisins</u> or <u>sultanas</u>

<u>Salt and pepper</u>

2 tsp <u>curry powder</u> or <u>paste</u>

Shredded <u>lettuce</u>

<u>Tomato</u> wedges

SERVE WITH

<u>Crusty bread</u>

Tofu- &
tvp-based dishes

Firm tofu, or soya bean curd, makes a great alternative to meat or cheese in recipes. Dried soya mince (TVP) is incredibly cheap and very nutritious, being high in protein and very low in fat. It virtually trebles in weight when reconstituted, so you need only ⅓ mug of dried soya for every mugful of minced (ground) meat or Quorn. You simply reconstitute it with water before use following packet directions. You'll find it with the dried pulses in the supermarket.

I haven't included any recipes using soya chunks because I don't find they give very tasty results, but feel free to experiment with them instead of mince, or throw them in any of the vegetable recipes – they, too, are very cheap.

Sweet & sour tofu

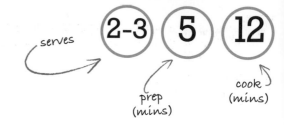

serves 2-3 — prep (mins) 5 — cook (mins) 12

Make this go round for one or two more people by adding more peas and a couple of grated carrots to the mixture, then serving it with lots of extra boiled or fried rice and perhaps some prawn crackers, if you eat them.

Knob of <u>butter</u> or <u>margarine</u>

1 tbsp <u>oil</u>

250 g packet <u>firm tofu</u>, cubed

300 g/1 small can <u>broken mandarin orange segments</u> (they're cheaper than whole ones)

½ mug <u>frozen peas</u>

½ tsp <u>ground ginger</u>

1 tbsp <u>light brown sugar</u>

1 tbsp <u>soy sauce</u>

1 tbsp <u>vinegar</u>

1 tbsp <u>tomato purée</u>

½ tsp <u>garlic</u> from a jar or tube

1 tbsp <u>cornflour</u>

1 tbsp <u>water</u>

SERVE WITH

<u>Plain boiled rice</u>

1 Heat the butter or margarine and oil in a large frying pan and fry the tofu for about 5 minutes, stirring, until golden. Remove from the pan and drain on kitchen paper.

2 Drain the mandarin orange segments, reserving the juice in a mug. Fill to the top of the mug with water. Stir into the frying pan with the mandarin oranges, peas, tofu and the remaining ingredients except the cornflour and water. Bring to the boil and simmer for 3 minutes.

3 Blend the cornflour with the water and stir into the pan. Cook, stirring, for 2 minutes until thickened. Taste and add more soy sauce if liked.

4 Serve on a bed of boiled rice.

Vegetarian chilli

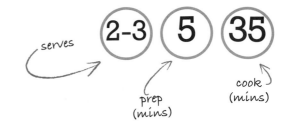

serves 2-3
prep (mins) 5
cook (mins) 35

Turn this into enchiladas by spooning it on to flour tortillas, rolling them up and putting them in an ovenproof dish. Smother with grated cheese and bake in a hot oven until the cheese bubbles, about 15 minutes. Good in crispy tacos too.

½ mug dried soya mince
Boiling water
2 tsp oil
1 small onion, chopped
2 tbsp tomato purée
½ tsp garlic from a jar or tube
½ tsp chilli powder (or less if you don't like much fire)
½ tsp ground cumin (optional)
½ tsp dried mixed herbs
425 g/1 large can red kidney beans, including the liquid
½ mug water
1 tbsp Marmite, or other yeast extract
Salt and pepper
SERVE WITH
Shredded lettuce and rice or rolled up flour tortillas

1 Put the soya mince in a bowl and just cover with boiling water. Stir. Leave to stand until ready to use.

2 Heat the oil in a saucepan and fry the onion for 2 minutes, stirring, until softened and lightly golden.

3 Add the soaked mince and the remaining ingredients and stir well. Bring to the boil, reduce the heat to moderate and simmer for 20–30 minutes, stirring occasionally, until the mince and beans are bathed in a rich sauce. If the mixture still looks slightly runny, boil rapidly for a minute or so. Taste and re-season if necessary.

4 Serve in bowls, surrounded by shredded lettuce with rice or rolled up flour tortillas.

Tofu & bean stir-fry

serves **2** prep (mins) **5** cook (mins) **12**

To make this go round for a couple more people, simply double the quantity of vegetables and flavourings. Omit the chilli if you prefer a milder flavour. Use a pack of marinated tofu pieces for a more intense taste.

1 Heat the oil in a wok or large frying pan. Add the beans, carrot and pepper and stir-fry for 5 minutes. (If using canned beans, add them for the last minute of stir-frying only.)

2 Stir in the remaining ingredients, bring to the boil and cook for 7 minutes, stirring occasionally.

3 Serve straight away with boiled rice, noodles or bread.

2 tbsp <u>oil</u>

200 g <u>green beans</u>, topped and tailed and cut into 3 pieces (or use frozen or drained canned beans)

1 large <u>carrot</u>, cut into matchsticks

1 small <u>red pepper</u> (optional), cut into strips

250 g/1 packet <u>firm tofu</u>, cubed

1 tbsp <u>light brown sugar</u>

1 tbsp <u>vinegar</u>

1 tbsp <u>soy sauce</u>

$1/4$ tsp <u>chilli powder</u>

$2/3$ mug <u>boiling water</u>

$1/2$ <u>vegetable stock cube</u>

SERVE WITH

<u>Boiled rice</u>, <u>noodles</u> or <u>bread</u>

Marinated
tofu kedgeree

This is ideal when you're feeding a few mates. To make it go round for more people, cook a handful of extra rice per person (and up the curry powder a bit), add some more peas and perhaps another hard-boiled egg.

1 mug long-grain rice

2 eggs, scrubbed under the cold tap

Salt

Knob of butter or margarine

1 onion, chopped

150 g packet marinated tofu pieces

1 mug frozen peas

1 tsp curry powder

1. Cook the rice and unshelled eggs in plenty of lightly salted boiling water for 10 minutes until the rice is just tender. Drain into a colander. Put the eggs in cold water.

2. Heat the butter or margarine in the saucepan and fry the onion for 3 minutes until soft and lightly golden.

3. Add the tofu and peas and fry, stirring, for 4–5 minutes until the peas are tender.

4. Stir in the curry powder, then add the rice and toss well.

5. Shell the eggs and cut in quarters. Add to the pan and toss over a gentle heat until piping hot.

Potato & tofu sauté

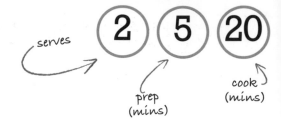

serves 2
prep (mins) 5
cook (mins) 20

This is good served with a sprinkling of soy, vegetarian Worcestershire or brown table sauce and a crisp green salad on the side. If you use ordinary new potatoes, just scrub them in cold water before cutting.

8 washed salad potatoes, cut into bite-sized pieces

A large knob of butter or margarine

1 tbsp olive oil

4 spring onions, chopped

1 small green pepper, halved and sliced

200 g/1 small can sweetcorn, drained

250 g block of firm tofu, cubed

½ tsp dried mixed herbs

Salt and pepper

1 Boil the potatoes in lightly salted water until just tender, about 8–10 minutes. Drain.

2 Heat the butter and oil in a frying pan or wok. Add the spring onions and green pepper and stir-fry for 2 minutes.

3 Add the potatoes and continue to fry, stirring and turning, for 5 minutes until turning golden.

4 Add the remaining ingredients to the pan, season to taste with salt and pepper and continue to cook, stirring and turning, for 3 minutes until everything is piping hot. Serve straight from the pan.

Vegetarian bolognese

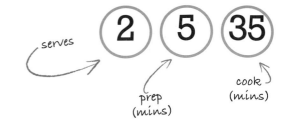

serves **2**
prep (mins) **5**
cook (mins) **35**

If you've any dregs of wine lurking in the kitchen, slosh it in. You'll then need to boil the mixture rapidly for a couple of minutes at the end of cooking to reduce the liquid.

½ mug dried soya mince
Boiling water
2 tsp oil
1 onion, chopped
1 tbsp tomato purée
1 tsp garlic from a jar or tube
400 g/1 large can tomatoes
1 tsp caster (superfine) sugar
½ tsp dried mixed herbs, oregano
or basil
Salt and pepper
¼–⅓ x 500 g packet spaghetti
SERVE WITH
Grated Parmesan-style cheese,
suitable for vegetarians and
salad

1 Put the soya mince in a bowl and just cover with boiling water. Stir. Leave to stand until ready to use.

2 Meanwhile, heat the oil in a saucepan and fry the onion for 2 minutes, stirring, until it is slightly softened.

3 Add the soaked soya mince and the remaining ingredients, except the spaghetti, and break up the tomatoes with a wooden spoon.

4 Bring to the boil, reduce the heat and simmer over a moderate heat for 20–30 minutes, stirring occasionally, until the mixture has formed a rich sauce. Taste and re-season if necessary.

5 Meanwhile, cook the spaghetti in plenty of boiling, lightly salted water (see page 18). Drain and divide between serving plates.

6 Spoon the sauce over and serve with grated cheese and salad.

Vegetarian lasagne

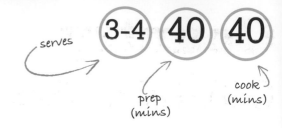

serves **3-4**
prep (mins) **40**
cook (mins) **40**

If you like lots of sauce, double the quantities of flour, milk, butter or margarine and cheese. Any leftovers can be reheated the next day in the microwave or are good eaten cold.

3 tbsp plain flour
1 mug milk
Knob of butter or margarine
½ mug grated Cheddar cheese
Salt and pepper
1 quantity of Vegetarian spaghetti bolognese sauce (see page 81)
6-8 no-need-to-precook lasagne sheets
SERVE WITH
Salad

1 Put the flour in a small saucepan and whisk in the milk until smooth. Add the butter or margarine. Bring to the boil, whisking all the time, until thickened and smooth. Cook for 2 minutes, still whisking.

2 Stir in the cheese and season to taste. Add a dash more milk if slightly to thick. It should be a thick, pouring consistency.

3 Preheat the oven to 190°C/375°F/gas 5/fan oven 170°C.

4 Put a thin layer of the sauce in a fairly shallow, ovenproof dish. Top with a layer of lasagne sheets, breaking them to fit. Repeat thin layers of sauce and lasagne, finishing with lasagne. Spoon the cheese sauce over.

5 Bake in the oven for about 35 minutes until golden and bubbling, and the lasagne feels tender when a knife is inserted down through the centre.

almost finished

6 Serve hot with salad.

Country cottage pie

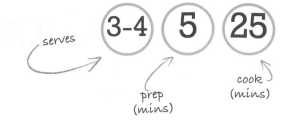

serves 3-4

prep (mins) 5

cook (mins) 25

If you are in a hurry you could use instant mash. Don't make it too wet though or it tends to 'melt' when baked. If you have a flameproof casserole, use this to cook and serve the soya mixture in to save washing up.

⅓ mug dried soya mince
Boiling water
2 tsp oil
1 onion, chopped
3 carrots, finely chopped
½ mug frozen peas
1 mug boiling water
1 vegetable stock cube
2 tsp Marmite, or other yeast extract
½ tsp dried mixed herbs
2 tbsp plain flour
2 tbsp cold water
Salt and pepper
3 large potatoes, cut into small pieces
Butter or margarine
1 tbsp milk

1 Put the soya mince in a bowl and just cover with boiling water. Stir and leave to stand until ready to use.

2 Heat the oil in a saucepan and fry the onion for 2 minutes, stirring.

3 Add the soya mince, carrots, peas, stock, Marmite and herbs. Bring to the boil, part-cover, reduce the heat and simmer for 15–20 minutes until the carrots are really tender.

4 Blend the flour with the cold water until smooth. Stir into the pan and cook for 2 minutes until thickened. Taste and season as necessary. Turn into a flameproof dish.

5 Meanwhile, cook the potatoes in boiling, lightly salted water until tender. Drain and mash with a knob of butter or margarine and milk. Spoon on top of the soya mixture, then dot with a little more butter or margarine. Place under a hot grill until golden brown.

Pulse-based dishes

Dried peas, beans and lentils are a vegetarian's best friend. They're cheap, nutritious and very filling! I've called for cans of them in most recipes because I'm naturally lazy, but if you want to make mega savings, buy a packet of dried beans, soak them in cold water, then boil rapidly for 10 minutes, to destroy any toxins in them, then reduce the heat and simmer so they are gently bubbling for 45 minutes to 1 hour, depending on the type, until they are tender. Don't add salt or you'll toughen them. Top up with more boiling water during cooking if necessary. Once cooked, drain, cool and store in a covered container in the fridge for several days to use as required, or pack in plastic bags in usable amounts. (A 450 g pack of dried beans is the equivalent of 4 x 425 g/large cans.)

Spiced bean tacos

This is just spiced up baked beans but they do taste very good! You could use a can of refried beans instead of baked beans in tomato sauce for a more authentic dish!

2 tbsp oil
1 small onion, chopped
½ tsp chilli powder
400 g/1 large can baked beans
2 tomatoes, chopped
5 cm piece of cucumber, chopped
Salt and pepper
12 taco shells
Grated Cheddar cheese

1 Heat the oil in a frying pan and fry the onion for 2 minutes.

2 Add the chilli powder and beans, and mash the beans well with a potato masher. Cook for 2 minutes.

3 Stir in the tomatoes and cucumber and season to taste.

4 Warm the taco shells according to the packet instructions.

5 Spoon the mixture into the taco shells, top with some grated cheese and serve straight away.

Cheesy lentil croquettes

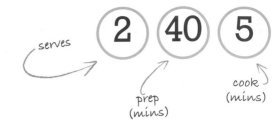

serves **2** prep (mins) **40** cook (mins) **5**

To use the rest of the stuffing, try dipping slices of aubergine in beaten egg then the stuffing mix and frying in hot oil until golden on both sides. Serve with plain yoghurt flavoured with dried mint and a little chopped cucumber.

1 onion, finely chopped
½ mug red lentils
1 full mug water
¼ tsp dried mixed herbs
½ mug grated cheddar cheese
1 mug fresh wholemeal breadcrumbs
1 egg, separated
Salt and pepper
½ x 85 g/1 small packet sage and onion stuffing mix
Oil, for shallow-frying
½ mug passata
SERVE WITH
Crisp salad

1 Put the onion, lentils and water in a saucepan. Bring to the boil, then reduce the heat until just bubbling gently round the edges. Cook for about 30 minutes or until the lentils are tender and have absorbed all the liquid, stirring frequently to prevent sticking.

2 Stir in the herbs, parsley, cheese, breadcrumbs, the egg yolk and some salt and pepper. Tip out into a shallow dish, spread out and leave to cool.

3 Divide into eight equal portions and roll each into a sausage shape.

4 Put the stuffing mix in a shallow dish. Lightly beat the egg white with a fork on a separate plate.

5 Dip the rolls in the egg white, then turn over in the stuffing mix to coat completely.

6 Heat about 5 mm oil in a frying pan. When hot, but not smoking, fry the rolls for 4–5 minutes turning until golden on all sides. Drain on kitchen paper.

7 Warm the passata in a saucepan or in a bowl in the microwave. Spoon over the croquettes and serve with a crisp salad.

almost finished

Chick pea & mushroom goulash

serves **2**

prep (mins) **5**

cook (mins) **9**

I've suggested serving this just with crusty bread but you could pile it on pasta or rice to make it more substantial. If you can't be bothered to make a full salad, slice some cucumber, toss it in a little vinegar and sprinkle with pepper.

1 small onion, finely chopped

1 tbsp oil

8 cup mushrooms, quartered

2 tomatoes, chopped

425 g/1 large can chick peas, drained

2 tsp tomato ketchup

2 tsp vegetarian Worcestershire sauce

2 tsp paprika

¼ tsp chilli powder (optional)

2 spoonfuls crème fraîche or plain yoghurt (optional)

SERVE WITH

Crusty bread and a green salad

1 In a saucepan, fry the onion in the oil for 2 minutes, stirring, until softened. Add the mushrooms and tomatoes and cook, stirring, for 2 minutes.

2 Add the remaining ingredients except the crème fraîche or yoghurt and simmer, stirring, for about 5 minutes or until the mushrooms are just cooked but most of the liquid has evaporated, stirring occasionally.

3 Serve in bowls, topped with a spoonful of crème fraîche or yoghurt, if liked, with crusty bread.

Vegetable & lentil stir-fry

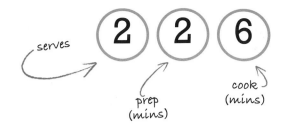

serves **2**

prep (mins) **2**

cook (mins) **6**

This is one to make when you can buy fresh ready-prepared stir-fry vegetables reduced for quick sale. If eating alone, store the rest of the stir-fry in the fridge and reheat (or eat cold) the next day.

1 or 2 slabs <u>Chinese egg noodles</u>

2 tbsp <u>sunflower oil</u>

225 g packet fresh mixed <u>stir-fry vegetables</u>

425 g/1 large can <u>green</u> or <u>brown lentils</u>, drained

2 tbsp bottled <u>black bean sauce</u>

1 tbsp <u>soy sauce</u>

1 tbsp <u>apple juice</u> or <u>cider</u> (if you have it around)

1 Cook the noodles according to the packet directions. Drain thoroughly.

2 Heat the oil in a large frying pan or wok. Add the vegetables and stir-fry for 2 minutes.

3 Add the cooked noodles and lentils and toss for 1 minute.

4 Add the sauces and apple juice or cider and toss again. Serve in bowls.

Cheesy dhal

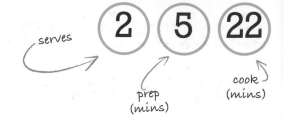

serves → **2** **5** **22**

prep (mins)

cook (mins)

Warm the bread briefly under the grill or in a microwave before serving. Try this with paneer, the mild Indian cheese, available in supermarkets, for a change from Cheddar or Edam.

Large knob of <u>butter</u> or <u>margarine</u>
1 tbsp <u>sunflower oil</u>
1 <u>onion</u>, chopped
1 tsp mild <u>curry powder</u> or <u>paste</u>
½ mug <u>red lentils</u>
1 mug <u>water</u>
1 <u>vegetable stock cube</u>
1 <u>bay leaf</u>
<u>Salt and pepper</u>
5 cm chunk of mild <u>Cheddar</u> or <u>Edam cheese</u>, cubed
A little chopped <u>fresh coriander</u> or <u>parsley</u> (optional)
SERVE WITH
<u>Garlic and coriander naan bread</u>
<u>Sticks of raw vegetables</u>

1 Heat the butter or margarine in a saucepan. Add the onion and cook, stirring, for 2 minutes.

2 Stir in the remaining ingredients except the cheese and coriander. Cook until bubbling, then turn down the heat, cover and cook gently for 20 minutes, stirring occasionally, until the lentils are tender and have absorbed the liquid, adding a little more water, if necessary.

3 Stir in the cheese and continue to heat until the cheese is just beginning to melt.

4 Spoon the dhal into a bowl, sprinkle with the coriander or parsley, if using, and serve straight away with the naan bread and raw vegetable sticks.

Baked lentils with **cheese**

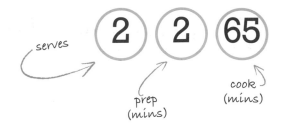

serves **2**

prep (mins) **2**

cook (mins) **65**

If you want to cook this in the evening, put the lentils in a bowl of cold water before you go to lectures in the morning, then it'll be ready to cook when you get back.

1 mug <u>brown</u> or <u>green lentils</u>, soaked for at least 2 hours

½ tsp <u>garlic</u> from a jar or tube

1 tbsp <u>tomato ketchup</u>

2 tsp <u>sweet pickle</u> or <u>brown table sauce</u>

1 tsp <u>soy sauce</u>

<u>Salt and pepper</u>

1 mug grated <u>Cheddar cheese</u>

SERVE WITH

<u>Green salad</u>

1 Drain the soaked lentils and place in a small flameproof casserole or saucepan. Cover with water, bring to the boil, reduce the heat, part-cover and simmer for about 45 minutes until tender.

2 Preheat the oven to 200°C/400°F/gas 6/fan oven 180°C.

3 Drain the lentils and return to the casserole or, if cooked in a saucepan, transfer to an ovenproof dish. Stir in the remaining ingredients, adding about three-quarters of the cheese. Sprinkle the remaining cheese on top.

4 Bake in the oven for about 20 minutes until turning golden on top.

5 Serve with a green salad.

Red bean nachos

This is great at a party. If eating alone, fill as many tortilla chips as you want, store the rest of the filling in the fridge and seal the bag of chips with a peg or some sticky tape so they don't go soft, then use within three days.

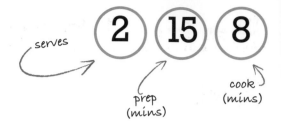

serves 2
prep (mins) 15
cook (mins) 8

425 g/1 large can <u>red kidney beans</u>, drained

2 tsp <u>dried minced onion</u> or ½ grated small fresh one

1 tsp <u>chilli powder</u>

1 tbsp <u>tomato purée</u>

Good pinch of <u>caster (superfine) sugar</u>

<u>Pepper</u>

200 g/1 large packet <u>corn tortilla chips</u>

4–6 handfuls of grated <u>Cheddar cheese</u>

1 Preheat the oven to 200°C/400°F/gas 6/fan oven 180°C.

2 Mash the beans with a fork in a bowl. Work in the onion, chilli, tomato purée and sugar. Add a good grinding of pepper.

3 Spread a little mixture on each tortilla chip and lay them on a large baking sheet or use a shallow ovenproof dish.

4 Sprinkle with the cheese and bake in the oven for about 8 minutes until the cheese has melted and is bubbling. Serve straight away.

Baked bean loaf

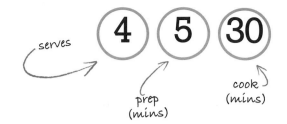

serves 4
prep (mins) 5
cook (mins) 30

Most people wouldn't think of turning baked beans into a loaf but they do taste remarkably good! The remainder is delicious served cold the next day with French bread and pickles.

400 g/1 large can <u>baked beans</u>

1 small <u>onion</u>, chopped

2 slices of <u>bread</u>, crumbled

2 tbsp <u>tomato ketchup</u>

1 <u>egg</u>, beaten

1 tsp <u>Marmite</u>, or other <u>yeast extract</u>

1 tsp <u>dried mixed herbs</u>

<u>Salt and pepper</u>

SERVE WITH

<u>Potatoes</u>, <u>carrots</u> and <u>vegetarian gravy</u> (see page 105)

1 Preheat the oven to 180°C/350°F/gas 4/fan oven 160°C.

2 Put all the ingredients in a bowl and mix well. Turn the mixture into a greased 450 g loaf tin, preferably lined with greased, greaseproof paper, or a greased, ovenproof dish.

3 Bake in the oven for about 30 minutes or until the mixture feels set to the touch.

4 Cool slightly, then loosen the edges with a round-bladed knife and turn out of the tin (don't bother if in a dish).

5 Serve cut into slices (or serve cut in wedges straight from the dish) with potatoes, carrots and vegetarian gravy.

Mixed bean salad

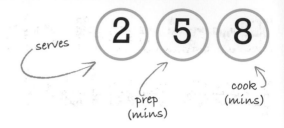

serves **2**
prep (mins) **5**
cook (mins) **8**

If you don't want to hard-boil eggs, beat them with a splash of milk and a pinch of dried mixed herbs, fry them in a pan to make a thin omelette, then roll it up and cut in shreds to top the salad.

2 eggs
½ small <u>onion</u> or 2 <u>spring onions</u>, chopped
¼ tsp <u>garlic</u> from a jar or tube
2 tbsp <u>sunflower</u> or <u>olive oil</u>
2 tsp <u>vinegar</u>
<u>Salt and pepper</u>
425 g/1 large can <u>red kidney beans</u>, drained
300 g/1 small can <u>broad beans</u>, drained
300 g/1 small can cut <u>green beans</u>, drained
<u>Lettuce leaves</u>
SERVE WITH
<u>Crusty bread</u>

1 Put the eggs in water, cover with a lid. Bring to the boil and boil for 6 minutes. Drain and cover with cold water.

2 Whisk the onion, garlic purée, oil, vinegar and a little salt and pepper in a bowl. Add the drained beans and toss gently but well.

3 Shell the eggs and chop.

4 Pile the bean mixture on to lettuce leaves on plates and top with the chopped egg.

5 Serve with crusty bread.

Braised chick pea salad

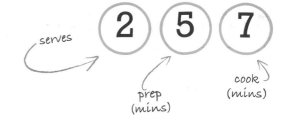

serves **2** prep (mins) **5** cook (mins) **7**

This is good hot with rice, couscous or pasta too. It's worth using olive oil if you like it and drizzling a bit extra over before serving. Try throwing in a few olives as well.

1 Put all the ingredients except the cheese in a saucepan. Bring to the boil and boil fairly rapidly for about 5 minutes until the chick peas are bathed in sauce.

2 Turn into a bowl, leave until cold, then chill in the fridge.

3 Serve in bowls sprinkled with Feta cheese, if liked, with crusty bread and a green salad.

1 onion, chopped
2 tbsp olive oil
400 g/1 large can tomatoes
1 tbsp tomato purée
1 tbsp garlic from a jar or tube
½ tsp dried mixed herbs
1 tbsp vinegar
430 g/1 large can chick peas, drained
Salt and pepper
A little crumbled Feta cheese (optional)
SERVE WITH
Crusty bread and a green salad

Roasts & burgers

Non-vegetarians often have a strange concept of nut roasts and the like. They think they're 'cranky'. They're not, they're absolutely delicious and a great way of filling up lots of people with lots of goodness. If you like your food moist, there are a couple of recipes for vegetarian gravy in this section or you could always heat a can of tomatoes, well mashed, to form a chunky sauce or buy a jar of passata for a smooth alternative. But remember to keep it in the fridge once opened or it'll go off. A final choice would be to heat a can of condensed mushroom, tomato or celery soup, thin with milk to the consistency you like and serve that with the roast.

Simple nut roast

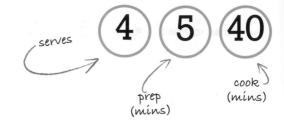

serves

4 5 40

prep (mins)

cook (mins)

Prepare your vegetables for roasting and put them in the oven on the top shelf before you prepare the nut roast. Then they'll all be ready to eat at about the same time.

2 tsp <u>Marmite</u>, or other <u>yeast extract</u>

⅔ mug <u>boiling water</u>

1¼ mugs <u>chopped mixed nuts</u>

3 slices of <u>wholemeal bread</u>, crumbled

1 small <u>onion</u>, finely chopped

4 tsp <u>soy sauce</u>

½ tsp <u>dried mixed herbs</u>

2 tbsp melted <u>butter</u> or <u>margarine</u>

1 tsp <u>oil</u>

<u>Salt and pepper</u>

SERVE WITH

<u>Roast potatoes, carrots and parsnips</u> (see page 17) and <u>mushroom gravy</u> (see page 105) or any of the suggestions on previous page

1 Preheat the oven to 190°C/375°F/gas 5/fan oven 170°C.

2 Dissolve the Marmite in the water in a large bowl. Add the remaining ingredients and mix thoroughly.

3 Turn into a greased 450 g loaf tin or ovenproof dish and press down gently.

4 Roast in the oven for 30–40 minutes until crisp on top and hot through.

5 Serve with roast vegetables and mushroom gravy.

Spinach & nut **roast**

serves 4 prep (mins) 10 cook (mins) 60

This is quick to make and nutritious too. I suggest serving it with warm passata but you could serve the vegetarian gravy on page 105 instead. Eat the rest cold with a tomato salad. Smallish potatoes cook quicker.

¼ x 1 kg bag frozen chopped spinach, thawed

1 large onion, grated

1 tsp garlic from a jar or tube

1 full mug chopped mixed nuts

4 slices wholemeal bread, crumbled

1 tsp dried mixed herbs

1 egg

1 tsp Marmite, or other yeast extract

Salt and pepper

SERVE WITH

Jacket potatoes, warm passata (you'll need about half a jar for four servings, just a few tablespoons for one) and sweetcorn

1 Preheat the oven to 180°C/350°F/gas 4/fan oven 160°C.

2 Squeeze the spinach to remove a little of the water but not too dry. Mix with the onion, garlic, nuts bread and herbs.

3 Beat the egg with the marmite and stir in with some salt and pepper. Press the mixture into a greased 450 g loaf tin or ovenproof dish. Cover with greased foil.

4 Bake in the oven for about 1 hour until firm to the touch.

5 Turn out if in a loaf tin. Serve with jacket potatoes, warm passata spooned over and some sweetcorn.

Curried soya bean **roast**

serves **4** **15** **60**

prep (mins)

cook (mins)

This one has a nice depth of flavour. I like it with mango chutney and a cucumber raita – chopped cucumber mixed with plain yoghurt, a little garlic and some dried mint, and naan bread.

1 large <u>onion</u>, chopped

1 tbsp <u>oil</u>, plus extra for greasing

1 <u>carrot</u>, grated

1 <u>potato</u>, grated

1 tbsp <u>curry paste</u> or <u>powder</u>

1 slice of <u>bread</u>, crumbled

1 tbsp <u>mango chutney</u> or <u>sweet pickle</u>

425 g/1 large can <u>soya beans</u>, drained and mashed

1 <u>egg</u>, beaten

<u>Salt and pepper</u>

1 <u>Weetabix</u>, crushed

SERVE WITH

A little warmed <u>passata</u>

1 Fry the onion in the oil, stirring, for 2 minutes to soften.

2 Mix in the remaining ingredients except the Weetabix, seasoning to taste.

3 Preheat the oven to 190°C/375°F/gas 5/fan oven 170°C. Oil a 450 g loaf tin or ovenproof dish. Sprinkle with the Weetabix. Spoon in the soya mixture and press down firmly. Cover the tin or dish with oiled foil.

4 Bake in the oven for about 1 hour until firm to the touch. Cool slightly. Turn out if in a tin.

5 Serve in slices or wedges with warm passata.

Sage & onion **roast**

serves 4 · prep (mins) 10 · cook (mins) 40

This is another roast that is good served cold, particularly with sweet pickle, beetroot and a salad. The cheapest beans are cans of red kidney beans in supermarket economy ranges.

2 tbsp oil

2 onions, chopped

2 x 425 g/2 large cans any dried beans or lentils, drained

1 mug chopped mixed nuts

1 mug grated Edam or mild Cheddar cheese

1 tsp dried sage

1 tsp Marmite or other yeast extract

2 eggs, beaten

Salt and pepper

SERVE WITH

Roast potatoes, a green vegetable and vegetarian gravy (see page 105)

1 Preheat the oven to 190°C/375°F/gas 5/fan oven 170°C.

2 Heat the oil in a large saucepan and fry the onions for 2 minutes, stirring.

3 Add the drained beans or lentils and mash thoroughly with a fork or potato masher.

4 Stir in the remaining ingredients and mix together well.

5 Turn into a greased 450 g/1 lb loaf tin or an ovenproof dish and press down lightly.

6 Roast in the oven for about 30–40 minutes or until the mixture feels set when lightly pressed. Leave to cool slightly, then turn out if in a tin.

almost finished

7 Serve with roast potatoes, a green vegetable and vegetarian gravy.

Veggie burgers

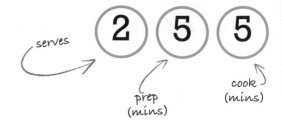

serves **2** prep (mins) **5** cook (mins) **5**

Shape the same mixture into four to six sausages and serve in finger rolls with fried onions, ketchup and mustard. You can even cheat and buy canned fried onions now!

½ mug <u>porridge oats</u>

½ mug <u>wholemeal flour</u>

2 <u>carrots</u>, grated

¼ mug grated <u>Cheddar cheese</u>

1 small <u>onion</u>, finely chopped

2 tsp <u>tomato purée</u>

2 tsp <u>soy sauce</u>

½ tsp <u>dried mixed herbs</u>

<u>Salt and pepper</u>

1 small <u>egg</u>, beaten

<u>Oil</u> for shallow frying

SERVE WITH

<u>Burger buns</u>, <u>salad</u> and <u>dill pickle</u> slices

1 Mix all the ingredients together except the egg and oil. Mix with enough of the egg to bind the ingredients together without making it too wet. Shape into 4 fairly flat burgers, using a little more flour if necessary.

2 Heat about 5 mm of oil in a large frying pan and fry the burgers for 5 minutes, turning once until cooked through and golden brown.

3 Serve in the traditional way with burger buns, salad and dill pickle slices.

Nutty bean burgers

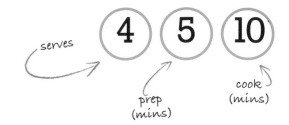

You can use whatever can of beans you have to hand for these. Omit the parsnip if preferred and double up on carrot. The nuts add a good texture. Use chopped peanuts if you prefer.

425 g/1 large can <u>red kidney</u>
<u>beans</u>, drained
1 <u>carrot</u>, grated
1 small <u>parsnip</u>, grated
¼ mug <u>chopped mixed nuts</u>
2 slices of <u>bread</u>, crumbled
1 tsp <u>Marmite</u>, or other <u>yeast</u>
<u>extract</u>
<u>Salt and pepper</u>
1 <u>egg</u>, beaten
<u>Oil</u> for shallow-frying
SERVE WITH
<u>Chips</u> and <u>salad</u>

1 Mash the beans well in a bowl. Add the remaining ingredients except the oil, using enough of the beaten egg to bind the mixture together without making it too wet.

2 Shape into 4 burgers and chill, if there is time, for 30 minutes.

3 Heat about 5 mm of hot oil in a frying pan and shallow-fry until golden brown on both sides. Drain on kitchen paper.

4 Serve with chips and salad.

Rough falafel

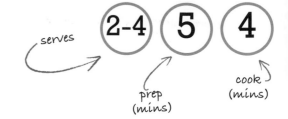

serves **2-4**

prep (mins) **5**

cook (mins) **4**

These tasty little burgers are really simple to make. If you have a hand blender you can purée the chick pea mixture first to make it smoother textured but it's not essential.

425 g/1 large can <u>chick peas</u>, drained

1 small <u>onion</u>, very finely chopped

1 tsp <u>garlic</u> from a jar or tube

½ tsp <u>chilli powder</u>

1 tsp <u>dried mint</u> (optional)

1 tsp <u>ground cumin</u> or <u>curry powder</u>

<u>Salt and pepper</u>

About 6 tbsp <u>plain flour</u>

1 <u>egg</u>, beaten

<u>Oil</u> for shallow-frying

4 <u>pitta breads</u>, warmed

<u>Shredded lettuce</u>

Slice of <u>cucumber</u> and <u>tomato</u>

Bought <u>tomato salsa</u>

1 Mash the chick peas well with a fork. Stir in the onion, garlic purée, chilli powder, mint and cumin or curry powder and season well.

2 Squeeze the mixture well with your hands so it sticks together, then shape into 8 balls and flatten slightly.

3 Coat with flour, then dip in beaten egg, then flour again.

4 Heat about 5 mm of oil in a frying pan and shallow-fry the falafel for about 4 minutes until golden, turning once. Drain on kitchen paper.

5 Split the pitta breads down one edge and open up to form pockets. Put 2 falafel in each pocket and add some lettuce, cucumber and tomato and some bought tomato salsa. Eat straight away.

TIP: If you don't mash the chick peas well enough, the mixture will be too coarse to stick together. If this happens, add the beaten egg to the mixture, omit the flour, then shallow-fry spoonfuls in hot oil.

Vegetarian
gravy

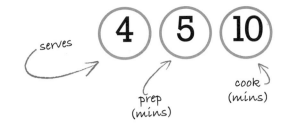

serves 4

prep (mins) 5

cook (mins) 10

This is worth making to pour over any of the roasts or even Quorn steaks. Try stuffing peppers or large mushrooms with a reconstituted packet stuffing, roasting them with about 1 cm water in a roasting tin, then serving with gravy.

1   Melt the butter or margarine and fry the onions for 5 minutes, stirring, until golden brown.

2   Stir in the flour, then blend in the remaining ingredients. Bring to the boil reduce the heat and simmer for 5 minutes, stirring all the time until thickened.

3   Either strain or leave in the onion bits and serve hot in a jug or gravy boat.

TIP: To make Mushroom gravy to serve with anything from nut roast to veggie sausage and mash, follow the recipe here but add 1 mug sliced or chopped mushrooms when the onions are half cooked, and don't strain at the end.

¼ x 250 g tub butter or margarine

2 onions, finely chopped

2 tbsp plain flour

1½ mugs boiling water

1 vegetable stock cube

1 tsp vegetarian Worcestershire sauce

1 tsp Marmite, or other yeast extract

Salt and pepper

Rice-based dishes

Rice comes in many shapes and forms. I've used ordinary long-grain for most of these recipes as it's the most economical. Obviously basmati and other more exotic sorts of rice have a terrific flavour and are worth using if you want to impress but you'll have to pay the price! If not eating the whole rice-based meal in one go, store it in the fridge as soon as it is cold. Don't leave it lying around at room temperature for hours – cooked rice is a good breeding ground for bacteria that can cause stomach upsets. If reheating, don't do so more than once and make sure it is piping hot through. Always check cooking times on the packet as they do vary.

Mushroom
risotto

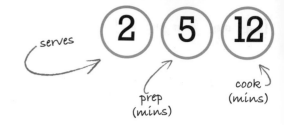

serves 2
prep (mins) 5
cook (mins) 12

This tarts up a packet of instant mushroom risotto and makes it very good indeed! Most people won't know you haven't slaved over the stove for ages adding a bit of stock at a time like you'd have to for the real thing!

250 g packet <u>mushroom risotto mix</u>
6 cups <u>mushrooms</u>, sliced
A knob of <u>butter</u> or <u>margarine</u>
4 tbsp <u>double cream</u>
<u>Pepper</u>
Grated <u>Parmesan-style cheese</u>, suitable for vegetarians

1 Make up the risotto according to the packet directions.

2 While it is cooking, cook the sliced mushrooms gently in the butter or margarine, stirring occasionally, for 5 minutes.

3 When the risotto is just cooked, stir in the mushrooms and their juices and the cream. Season with pepper. Spoon into warm shallow bowls and garnish with parsley.

4 Serve straight away sprinkled with grated Parmesan-style cheese.

Baked
vegetable risotto

As you use the oven for this, make enough for three or four. It's okay cold or can be reheated in the microwave (I usually add a dash of milk or water when reheating to moisten it). Alternatively, use the rest to stuff peppers (page 110).

3 tbsp oil
1 onion, chopped
⅔ mug long-grain rice
2 tsp curry powder
½ tsp chilli powder (optional)
1 carrot, chopped
1 green or red pepper, seeds removed and chopped
½ mug frozen peas
200 g/1 small can sweetcorn
Handful of pine nuts
1 tsp garlic from a jar or tube
1 vegetable stock cube
2 mugs boiling water
Salt and pepper

1 Preheat the oven to 180°C/350°F/gas 4/fan oven 160°C.

2 Heat the oil in a flameproof casserole or a saucepan.

3 Add the onion and fry for 2 minutes, stirring.

4 Add the rice and stir until coated with the oil, then add the remaining vegetables, pine nuts and garlic.

5 Dissolve the stock cube in the water and add. Stir well and bring to the boil.

6 If using a saucepan, tip into an ovenproof dish and cover with foil. If using a casserole, cover with the lid.

almost finished

7 Bake in the oven for 30–40 minutes until the rice and vegetables are tender and all the liquid has been absorbed. Stir well before serving.

Risotto-stuffed peppers

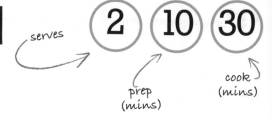

serves **2**

prep (mins) **10**

cook (mins) **30**

Serve with roasted roots. Put chunks of carrot, swede, baby potatoes, beetroot or whatever in a roasting tin. Trickle a little oil over, toss gently and sprinkle with salt. Put on the top shelf of the oven before you prepare the peppers.

2 <u>red</u> or <u>green peppers</u>

1 <u>egg</u>, beaten

About 1 mug leftover <u>cold cooked Baked vegetable risotto</u>

(see page 109)

1 Preheat the oven to 200°C/400°F/gas 6/fan oven 180°C.

2 Halve the peppers and remove the seeds.

3 Mix the beaten egg and risotto together and pack into the pepper halves.

4 Put them in a small baking tin containing about 5 mm of water. Cover with foil.

5 Bake in the oven for 30 minutes until the peppers are tender and the filling is piping hot.

6 Serve with the juices from the tin spooned over.

Tomato rice soup

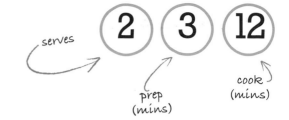

serves 2 3 12
prep (mins)
cook (mins)

This makes a filling and quick meal when times are hard. Adding the cheese gives you some protein, too, for a balanced meal. And it tastes much better than just a can or packet of soup.

Handful of long-grain rice
400 g/1 large can tomatoes
295 g/1 small can cream of tomato soup
vegetarian Worcestershire sauce
SERVE WITH
Grated Cheddar or Edam cheese
and crusty bread

1 Put the rice in a saucepan with the tomatoes and break them up with a wooden spoon.

2 Half-fill the tomato can with water and add to the pan. Bring to the boil, reduce the heat and simmer for 10 minutes until the rice is just tender, stirring occasionally.

3 Stir in the can of tomato soup and spike to taste with Worcestershire sauce. Heat through and serve with grated cheese and crusty bread.

Egg fried **rice**

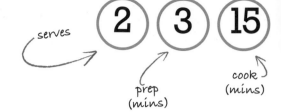

serves **2** **3** **15**

prep (mins)

cook (mins)

Make it more exciting by adding sliced courgettes or mushrooms. Fry these in the oil for a couple of minutes before adding the rice and peas. It's also good with a handful of raw peanuts, almonds or cashews thrown in.

½ mug long-grain rice

Salt

Handful of frozen peas

2 tbsp sunflower oil

2 eggs

A pinch of Chinese five spice powder (optional)

Soy sauce

1 Cook the rice in plenty of boiling, lightly salted water for 10 minutes, or according to packet directions, adding the peas half way through cooking. Drain in a colander, rinse with cold water and drain again thoroughly.

2 Heat the oil in a frying pan or wok.

3 Add the rice and peas and cook, stirring and turning, for 2 minutes.

4 Push the mixture to one side and tilt the pan. Pour in the beaten eggs.

5 Cook the egg, stirring, then gradually draw in the rice until it is filled with tiny strands of egg. Add a pinch of Chinese five-spice powder, if liked, and a sprinkling of soy sauce. Toss and serve.

Spanish rice

serves **2** **10** **22**

prep (mins)

cook (mins)

If you like, top this off with fried or poached eggs or serve it sprinkled with grated cheese. It's just as delicious cold the next day so cool it quickly and store it in a covered container in the fridge.

1 tbsp olive or sunflower oil
1 small green pepper, diced
1 onion, chopped
½ mug long-grain rice
1 vegetable stock cube
1¼ mugs boiling water
Salt and pepper
½ tsp dried oregano
¼ mug frozen peas
¼ mug frozen sweetcorn
1 tomato, chopped
A few sliced stoned olives

1 Heat the oil in a frying pan. Add the pepper and onion and stir-fry for 2 minutes.

2 Add the rice and stir until the grains are glistening with oil.

3 Dissolve the stock cube in a mugful of the water. Stir this and the remaining water into the rice with a little seasoning and the herbs. Bring to the boil, reduce the heat, cover with a lid or foil and cook over a low heat for 10 minutes.

4 Stir the rice, add the peas and sweetcorn, the tomato and the olives. Re-cover and cook for a further 10 minutes until the rice is cooked and has absorbed nearly all the liquid but is still moist. Taste and re-season if necessary.

Spinach & cheese rice

serves → 2 5 25
prep (mins)
cook (mins)

If you have some ground nutmeg, a pinch stirred in with the spinach gives it a great flavour. Try this with a little crumbled blue cheese instead of the Parmesan.

Knob of butter or margarine
1 tbsp oil
1 small onion, chopped
½ cup long-grain rice
1 vegetable stock cube
1¼ mugs boiling water
½ tsp dried mixed herbs or oregano
Salt and pepper
1 mug frozen chopped spinach, thawed
2 tbsp single cream
2 tbsp grated Parmesan-style cheese, suitable for vegetarians

1 Melt the butter or margarine with the oil in a saucepan. Add the onion and fry for 2 minutes, stirring.

2 Add the rice and stir until glistening.

3 Dissolve the stock cube in a mugful of the water. Add this, the remaining water, herbs and a little salt and pepper to the rice, stir well, bring to the boil, reduce the heat, cover and cook very gently for 15–20 minutes, stirring occasionally until tender and most of the liquid has been absorbed.

4 Add the spinach and cook for a further 3 minutes, stirring.

5 Stir in the cream. The rice should be soft and creamy, not dry and separate.

almost finished

6 Lastly stir in the cheese and re-season if necessary.

7 Serve hot straight from the pan.

Cashew paella

Cashew nuts are a bit extravagant but they taste fantastic. For a more economical dish, substitute peanuts. I love using a leek in this but you could use a chopped onion instead.

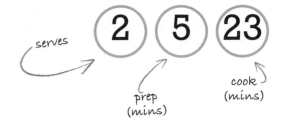

serves 2
prep (mins) 5
cook (mins) 23

1 tbsp oil
1 small leek, chopped
1 red pepper, chopped
4 mushrooms, sliced
½ mug long-grain rice
1 vegetable stock cube
1¼ mugs boiling water
Large handful of raw cashew nuts
Handful of frozen peas (optional)
¼ tsp dried mixed herbs
SERVE WITH
Salad

1 Heat the oil in a large pan and fry the vegetables over a gentle heat for 5 minutes, stirring.

2 Add the rice and stir until coated in oil.

3 Dissolve the stock cube in a mugful of the water. Add this, the remaining water and the remaining ingredients, bring to the boil, stirring, reduce the heat, cover and simmer gently for about 20 minutes until the rice is cooked and has absorbed the liquid. Stir gently once or twice.

4 Serve hot with salad.

Spicy fried rice & beans

serves **2**
prep (mins) **5**
cook (mins) **15**

This is fusion food – Caribbean style rice and peas, but fried in the Chinese way with Indian spices! Again, a great dish to do if you have cooked leftover rice from another meal.

1 Boil the rice in plenty of lightly salted water for 10 minutes, or according to packet directions. Drain in a colander, rinse with cold water and drain again.

2 Melt the butter or margarine in the rice saucepan, add the onion and spices and fry for 3 minutes.

3 Add the rice and beans and cook, stirring, for a few minutes until piping hot. Season to taste. Stir in the torn coriander leaves, if using.

4 Serve hot with cucumber raita, chutney and naan bread.

½ cup long-grain rice
Salt and pepper
Knob of butter or margarine
1 onion, finely chopped
2 tsp curry powder
¼ tsp chilli powder
425 g/1 large can black-eyed beans, drained
Handful of fresh coriander leaves, optional
SERVE WITH
Cucumber raita (chopped cucumber, mixed into yoghurt and flavoured with dried mint and a dash of garlic from a jar or tube), mango or other chutney and naan bread

Bean curd & ginger pilaf

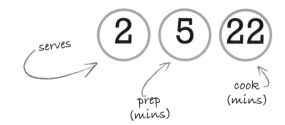

serves **2**

prep (mins) **5**

cook (mins) **22**

Here I've called for ground ginger, but fresh root ginger is actually better in most other Chinese-style recipes. If you're feeling flush, buy it ready-puréed in a jar or buy a piece of knobbly root which you peel and grate or chop finely and use instead.

Knob of <u>butter</u> or <u>margarine</u>
4 <u>spring onions</u> or 1 small <u>onion</u>, chopped
½ mug <u>long-grain rice</u>
½ tsp <u>ground ginger</u>
2 tsp <u>soy sauce</u>
¼ tsp <u>chilli powder</u>
1 <u>vegetable stock cube</u>
1¼ mugs <u>boiling water</u>
250 g/1 packet <u>firm tofu</u>, cubed
Large handful of <u>raisins</u>
SERVE WITH
Extra <u>soy sauce</u> and <u>satsumas</u> or similar fruit, segmented

1 Melt the butter or margarine in a saucepan. Add the onions and fry for 2 minutes, stirring.

2 Add the rice and stir to coat with butter or margarine. Stir in the ginger, soy sauce and chilli powder.

3 Dissolve the stock cube in a mugful of the water. Add this and the remaining water, bring to the boil, reduce the heat, cover and simmer very gently for 10 minutes.

4 Add the tofu and raisins and continue cooking for a further 10 minutes until the rice is tender and has absorbed the liquid.

Spoon on to warm plates and sprinkle a little extra soy sauce over. Scatter segments of satsuma over and serve.

almost finished

Veggie rice with egg

 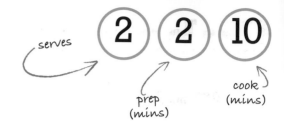

A simple meal for any day of the week. Throw in extras like a few sliced mushrooms, chopped pepper or courgettes as you please with the frozen vegetables.

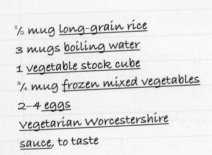

½ mug long-grain rice

3 mugs boiling water

1 vegetable stock cube

¾ mug frozen mixed vegetables

2–4 eggs

vegetarian Worcestershire sauce, to taste

1   Cook the rice in the boiling water to which the stock cube has been added for 5 minutes.

2   Add the vegetables and cook for a further 5 minutes until the vegetables are just tender. If the rice is not quite cooked, boil a minute or two more. Drain off excess liquid.

3   Meanwhile, poach the eggs (see page 15), or fry if you prefer.

4   Spoon the rice on to warm plates. Top with the eggs and add a good slosh of Worcestershire sauce.

Cuban rice **& eggs**

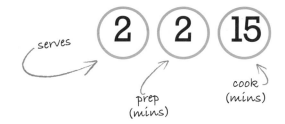

This is one of the exceptions to the eating cold the next day rule – eat and enjoy as soon as you've cooked it. If eating alone, cook half the quantity of rice, a small onion and banana and one or two eggs.

½ mug cup <u>long-grain rice</u>
1 <u>onion</u>, chopped
½ tsp <u>garlic</u> from a jar or tube
3 tbsp <u>oil</u>
Large pinch of <u>chilli powder</u>
1 not too ripe <u>banana</u>, cut into chunks
2–4 <u>eggs</u>
<u>Salt and pepper</u>
SERVE WITH
<u>Salad</u>

1 Cook the rice in plenty of boiling, salted water for 10 minutes or according to packet directions. Drain in a colander and keep warm over the saucepan with a little simmering water in it.

2 Meanwhile, fry the onion and garlic in 1 tbsp of the oil in a frying pan until golden brown. Stir in the chilli powder. Remove from the pan with a fish slice and add to the rice.

3 Add a further 1 tbsp of the oil to the frying pan and fry the banana, stirring, for about 2 minutes until just cooked but still holding its shape. Add to the rice.

4 Heat the remaining oil and fry the eggs. Mix the rice gently with the onions and banana, then season well.

5 Pile on to warm plates. Top each pile with 1 or 2 eggs and serve with salad.

Mushroom & nut pilaf

 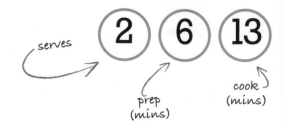
The peanuts add protein and a delicious texture. I prefer to use raw ones but you can use roasted, salted if you prefer (go even easier on the soy sauce though!).

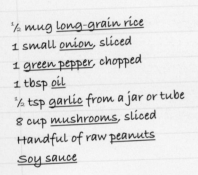

½ mug long-grain rice
1 small onion, sliced
1 green pepper, chopped
1 tbsp oil
½ tsp garlic from a jar or tube
8 cup mushrooms, sliced
Handful of raw peanuts
Soy sauce

1 Cook the rice in plenty of boiling, lightly salted water for 10 minutes or according to packet directions. Drain.

2 Meanwhile, fry the onion and pepper in the oil, stirring until softened and lightly golden, about 5 minutes.

3 Stir in the garlic, mushrooms and peanuts and fry for 1 minute.

4 Add the rice and stir well. Sprinkle with soy sauce to taste, remembering that it is very salty. Fry, stirring, for 2–3 minutes until heated through.

Brown rice & cheese salad

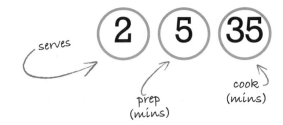

serves **2** prep (mins) **5** cook (mins) **35**

Brown rice has a chewy texture and nutty flavour. Use it instead of white for any of the recipes, just cook it for about 35 minutes until tender. To make this even more substantial, add a handful of nuts and/or raisins.

½ mug <u>brown rice</u>
½ mug <u>frozen mixed vegetables</u>
1 tbsp <u>oil</u>
2 tsp <u>vinegar</u>
<u>Salt and pepper</u>
Large handful of cubed <u>Cheddar cheese</u>
1 <u>eating apple</u>, cored and diced
1–2 tbsp <u>mayonnaise</u>

1 Cook the rice in plenty of boiling, salted water for about 30 minutes, or according to packet directions.

2 Add the vegetables and cook for a further 5 minutes or until tender. Drain in a colander, rinse with cold water and drain again.

3 Mix in the oil, vinegar and a little salt and pepper and pile into nests on serving plates.

4 Mix the cheese and apple with the mayonnaise and a little salt and pepper and spoon into the centres.

Curried rice **& bean salad**

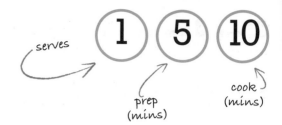

serves 1 · prep (mins) 5 · cook (mins) 10

I've given you the recipe from scratch but, if you are cooking rice as an accompaniment to another dish, cook twice as much as you need, and store it in the fridge to make this the following day. See page 107 for tips on storing rice safely.

⅓ mug long-grain rice
1 tsp mild curry paste or powder
1 tbsp mayonnaise
Small handful of sultanas or raisins
225 g/1 small can baked beans in tomato sauce
Small handful of roasted or raw peanuts
Salt and pepper

1 Cook the rice in plenty of boiling, lightly salted water for 10 minutes, or according to packet directions. Drain in a colander, rinse with cold water and drain again.

2 Mix the curry paste or powder with the mayonnaise in a bowl.

3 Stir in the beans, rice, sultanas or raisins and nuts. Season to taste with salt and pepper.

Spiced coconut rice **salad**

serves **2** — prep (mins) **5** — cook (mins) **10**

If you're not planning to eat all this at one meal, do not add the banana to the portion you're setting aside as it won't keep too well overnight. It's great with some sliced avocado in it, too.

½ mug <u>long-grain rice</u>
2 tsp <u>curry powder</u>
2 tbsp <u>mayonnaise</u>
Handful of <u>raisins</u>
¼ block <u>creamed coconut</u>, grated
or 2–3 tbsp <u>desiccated coconut</u>
200 g/1 small can <u>sweetcorn</u>,
drained
5 cm piece of <u>cucumber</u>, diced
1 <u>banana</u>, sliced and tossed in a
little <u>lemon juice</u> or <u>vinegar</u> to
prevent browning
SERVE WITH
<u>Popadoms</u>

1 Cook the rice in plenty of boiling, salted water for 10 minutes or according to packet directions. Drain in a colander, rinse with cold water and drain again.

2 Mix the curry powder and mayonnaise in a bowl.

3 Add the rice and the remaining ingredients and toss gently but thoroughly.

4 Serve with popadoms.

TIP: Cook popadoms in the microwave one at a time for 30 seconds, turning once half way through cooking, until puffed all over.

Pasta-based dishes

Pasta is a great filler – versatile and good for you, too. At its simplest, cooked until just tender, then tossed with a little butter or margarine and some grated cheese, it's fine (see the tips on page 18) but not very exciting. Here are some innovative but inexpensive and dead easy ways with Italy's best export. Look out for economy brands, they'll work perfectly well and are much cheaper than some of the more famous brands. Always check cooking instructions as different makes do vary.

Spaghetti
with lentils

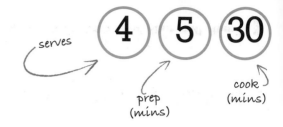

serves **4** prep (mins) **5** cook (mins) **30**

If you haven't got 4 people to feed, eat some today and use the rest spooned over boiled rice for another meal. You can add a pinch of dried oregano or mixed herbs instead of basil if you like.

⅔ mug green lentils
400 g/1 large can tomatoes
2½ mugs boiling water
1 vegetable stock cube
1 onion, chopped
1 tsp dried basil
Salt and pepper
⅓–½ x 500 g packet spaghetti
Grated Parmesan-style cheese, suitable for vegetarians

1 For best results, soak the lentils in cold water for several hours first, then drain before using. Put all the ingredients except the spaghetti and cheese in a large saucepan. Break up the tomatoes with a wooden spoon.

2 Bring to the boil, reduce the heat and simmer for about 30 minutes until the lentils are soft, stirring occasionally.

3 Meanwhile, cook the spaghetti in plenty of boiling, lightly salted water (see page 18) and drain. Pile on to plates and spoon the sauce over.

4 Sprinkle with grated cheese and serve.

Lasagne with ratatouille

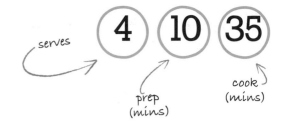

serves 4
prep (mins) 10
cook (mins) 35

If you like a really saucy lasagne, double the quantity of flour, milk, butter or margarine and cheese. For an even quicker sauce, beat an egg into a carton of crème fraîche, mix with cheese, salt and pepper and use that instead.

425 g/1 large can <u>ratatouille</u>
200 g/1 small can <u>sweetcorn</u>
½ tsp <u>dried mixed herbs</u>
6–8 sheets <u>no-need-to-precook</u>
<u>lasagne</u>
3 tbsp <u>plain flour</u>
1 mug <u>milk</u>
Knob of <u>butter</u> or <u>margarine</u>
<u>Salt and pepper</u>
2 large handfuls of grated
<u>cheddar cheese</u>
SERVE WITH
<u>Salad</u>

1 Preheat the oven to 190°C/375°F/gas 5/fan oven 170°C.

2 Mix the ratatouille, sweetcorn and herbs together.

3 Layer the mixture and the lasagne sheets in a shallow ovenproof dish, ending with a layer of lasagne.

4 Whisk the flour with the milk in a saucepan. Add the butter or margarine, bring to the boil and cook for 2 minutes, whisking all the time. Stir in half the cheese and season to taste.

5 Spoon the sauce over the lasagne and sprinkle with the remaining cheese.

6 Bake in the oven for about 35 minutes or until bubbling and golden brown. The lasagne should feel tender when a knife is inserted down through the centre.

7 Serve with salad.

Pasta bake with **eggs**

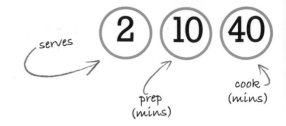

This makes a nice change from lasagne and can be put together in advance then baked half an hour before you are ready to eat.

¼ x 500 g packet <u>pasta shapes</u>
2 <u>eggs</u>, scrubbed under the cold tap
8 tbsp <u>passata</u>
½ tsp <u>dried basil</u> or <u>mixed herbs</u>
2 large handfuls of frozen <u>chopped spinach</u>, thawed
1 mug <u>milk</u>
3 tbsp <u>plain flour</u>
Knob of <u>butter</u> or <u>margarine</u>
2 large handfuls of grated <u>Cheddar cheese</u>
<u>Salt and pepper</u>

1 Cook the pasta and eggs in their shells in plenty of boiling water for 10 minutes or according to packet directions. Drain in a colander and plunge the eggs in cold water.

2 Preheat the oven to 200°C/400°F/gas 6/fan oven 180°C.

3 Put a layer of half the pasta in an ovenproof dish. Spoon half the passata over the pasta. Sprinkle with half of the basil or herbs and spread all the spinach over.

4 Shell the eggs and cut in slices. Lay over the spinach. Top with the remaining pasta then the remaining passata and sprinkle with the remaining herbs.

5 Whisk the milk and flour in the pasta saucepan until smooth. Add the butter or margarine and bring to the boil, whisking all the time. Cook for 2 minutes, whisking, until thickened. Add half the cheese and season to taste.

6 Pour over the pasta and top with the remaining cheese.

7 Cook in the oven for about 30 minutes or until golden brown and piping hot.

almost finished

Mushroom & walnut **pasta**

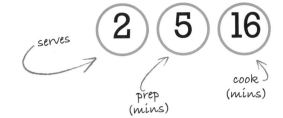

serves **2** prep (mins) **5** cook (mins) **16**

Walnut pieces are cheaper than halves because they're the broken ones. Nuts are a good source of protein so great to use in your cooking. You can use other varieties if you prefer.

¼ x 500 g packet <u>tagliatelle</u>

Knob of <u>butter</u> or <u>margarine</u>

1 <u>onion</u>, thinly sliced

6–8 <u>mushrooms</u>, sliced

⅓ cup <u>walnut pieces</u>, roughly chopped

1 small carton <u>crème fraîche</u>

½ tsp <u>dried mixed herbs</u>

<u>Salt and pepper</u>

SERVE WITH

<u>Tomato salad</u>

1 Cook the tagliatelle in boiling, lightly salted water according to the packet directions. Drain in a colander.

2 Melt the butter or margarine in the same pan and fry the onion for 4 minutes until soft and turning golden.

3 Add the mushrooms and fry for a further 2 minutes, stirring.

4 Add the remaining ingredients and heat through, stirring. Add the tagliatelle and toss well. Taste and re-season, if necessary.

5 Serve hot with a tomato salad.

Speedy pasta & **bean grill**

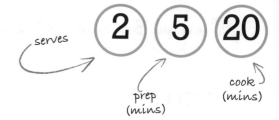

serves 2
prep (mins) 5
cook (mins) 20

It's easier to use the whole cans of beans and tomatoes so you may find it makes too much for two people (depending on your appetites). If so, reheat the rest the following day in the microwave in a covered dish.

¼ x 500 g packet <u>pasta shapes</u>
400 g/1 large can <u>tomatoes</u>
425 g/1 large can <u>red kidney beans</u>, drained
1 tsp <u>garlic</u> from a jar or tube
1 tsp <u>dried basil</u>
2 large handfuls of grated <u>Cheddar cheese</u>
Handful of <u>cornflakes</u> or <u>branflakes</u>, crushed
SERVE WITH
Shredded <u>white cabbage</u> tossed in a little <u>oil</u>, <u>vinegar</u>, <u>salt</u> and <u>pepper</u>

1   Cook the pasta according to the packet directions in a flameproof casserole (to save washing up) or a saucepan. Drain and return to the pan.

2   Add the tomatoes, breaking up well with a wooden spoon.

3   Add the beans, garlic, basil and some salt and pepper, toss gently and heat through until piping hot.

4   Preheat the grill. If using a saucepan, turn the mixture into a flameproof dish at this point. Sprinkle with the cheese and cornflakes. Place under a hot grill until golden and the cheese has melted.

5   Serve with a shredded cabbage salad.

Mushroom & pesto pasta

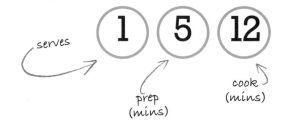

serves **1**
prep (mins) **5**
cook (mins) **12**

You can just stir the pesto into the spaghetti and leave out the mushrooms. To save washing up, cook the spaghetti, drain it in a colander, then cook the mushrooms in the same pan. Return the spaghetti and continue as step 3.

¹/₆–¹/₄ x 500g packet <u>spaghetti</u>
<u>Salt and pepper</u>
Knob of <u>butter</u> or <u>margarine</u>
4 cup <u>mushrooms</u>, sliced
1 small <u>onion</u>, finely chopped
2 tsp <u>pesto</u>
SERVE WITH
Grated <u>Parmesan-style cheese</u>, suitable for vegetarians and a <u>tomato salad</u>

1 Cook the spaghetti in boiling, lightly salted water for 10 minutes, or according to the packet directions. Drain and return to the saucepan.

2 Meanwhile, melt the butter or margarine in a frying pan, add the mushrooms and onion and cook for 3–4 minutes until soft and lightly golden.

3 Add the mushroom mixture to the pasta with the pesto and lift and stir lightly over a gentle heat until every strand is coated. Pile into a bowl and serve with Parmesan-style cheese and a tomato salad.

Spaghetti with broad beans

serves **2**

prep (mins) **5**

cook (mins) **10**

Use any long strands of pasta like linguine or tagliatelle instead of spaghetti. Frozen soya beans make a delicious alternative to broad beans. Add a little extra crème fraîche and reheat the other half in the microwave the next day.

⅓–½ x 500g packet <u>spaghetti</u> (according to appetites)
¼ x 1 kg bag frozen <u>baby broad beans</u>
Large knob of <u>butter</u> or <u>margarine</u>
1 <u>onion</u>, finely chopped
½ mug <u>boiling water</u>
½ <u>vegetable stock cube</u>
½ x 200 ml carton <u>crème fraîche</u>
Small handful of <u>fresh parsley</u>, chopped (optional)
4 tbsp grated <u>Parmesan-style cheese</u>, suitable for vegetarians

1 Cook the spaghetti in plenty of boiling, lightly salted water for 10 minutes or according to packet directions, adding the broad beans after 2 minutes. Drain, reserving ½ mug of the cooking water, and return the pasta and beans to the pan.

2 Meanwhile, melt the butter or margarine in another saucepan. Add the onion and fry, stirring over a gentle heat, for 3 minutes until softened but not browned. Add the reserved cooking water and the stock cube, bring to the boil and boil rapidly for about 4 minutes until reduced by half and slightly syrupy.

3 Stir in the crème fraîche, parsley, if using, and half the cheese. Add to the pasta and toss over a gentle heat until everything is coated in the sauce. Pile on to warm plates, sprinkle with the remaining cheese and serve.

Chinese noodles with **vegetables**

serves **2**

prep (mins) **2**

cook (mins) **5**

This is great when time is of the essence – it takes just minutes to put together and cook but tastes good. You can throw in a handful of peanuts for added texture and protein.

1 Cover the noodles with boiling water, stir well and leave to stand for 5 minutes.

2 Meanwhile, heat the drained vegetables in a pan.

3 Drain the noodles and add to the vegetables. Add the soy sauce and ginger, toss and serve.

2 slabs of Chinese egg noodles
425 g/1 large can Chinese stir-fry vegetables, drained
1 tbsp soy sauce
½ tsp ground ginger

Macaroni
cheese

serves

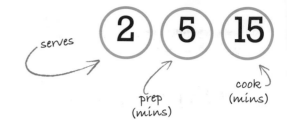

2 5 15

prep
(mins)

cook
(mins)

If you only have one pan, you'll have to cook the macaroni first and then make the sauce. I like it with some canned tomatoes, heated and served on the side or some grilled or fried fresh ones.

1 Cook the macaroni according to the packet directions. Drain and return to the saucepan.

2 Meanwhile, whisk the flour with a little of the milk in a separate saucepan until smooth. Whisk in the remaining milk and add the butter or margarine. Bring to the boil and boil for 2 minutes, whisking all the time, until thick and smooth.

3 Stir in the mustard and cheese and season to taste with salt and pepper. Add to the pasta and stir well.

4 Either serve straight away or spoon into a flameproof dish, top with the crumbled Weetabix or crushed bran flakes and sprinkle with a little extra grated cheese. Grill until golden and bubbling.

4 handfuls of <u>short-cut macaroni</u>

3 tbsp <u>plain flour</u>

1 mug <u>milk</u>

Large knob of <u>butter</u> or <u>margarine</u>

1 tsp <u>mustard</u> (optional)

2 large handfuls of grated <u>Cheddar cheese</u>

<u>Salt and pepper</u>

A <u>Weetabix</u> or a handful of <u>bran</u> or <u>corn flakes</u> and a little extra <u>grated cheese</u> (optional)

Tomato & basil pasta

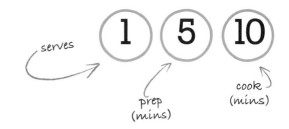

serves **1**   prep (mins) **5**   cook (mins) **10**

It's worth having a pot of fresh basil on the windowsill as it tastes great thrown into all sorts of dishes at the last minute, from pizzas to salads. You can use a good pinch of dried basil instead but the flavour won't be so good.

1 tbsp olive or sunflower oil
1 small onion, chopped
2 large ripe tomatoes, chopped
2 tsp tomato purée
A good pinch of sugar, salt and pepper
3 fresh basil leaves, chopped
⅙–¼ x 500 g packet spaghetti
Grated Parmesan-style cheese, suitable for vegetarians (optional) and a green salad

1 Heat the oil in a saucepan and add the onion. Cook, stirring, for 2 minutes.

2 Add the tomatoes, purée and seasoning, turn down the heat as low as possible, cover and cook over a for 5–10 minutes until pulpy, stirring occasionally.

3 Stir in the basil.

4 Meanwhile cook the spaghetti in boiling, salted water according to packet directions until just tender. Drain in a colander and return to the pan.

5 Add the tomato sauce and lift and stir to coat each strand in the sauce. Tip into a bowl and serve with grated cheese, if liked, and a green salad.

Pasta with corn & spinach

serves **2**

prep **5** (mins)

cook **12** (mins)

You can make the cheese sauce as for Macaroni cheese (page 134), put the hot pasta mixture in a flameproof dish, cover with the sauce, sprinkle with a little extra cheese and grill until golden and bubbling.

1 Cook the pasta according to the packet directions, drain and return to the pan.

2 Squeeze out the spinach to remove excess moisture. Mix with the pasta, tomatoes, sweetcorn, oregano and seasoning to taste. Heat through until piping hot.

3 Pile the pasta on to warm plates and sprinkle with grated cheese. Serve hot.

2 mugs of pasta shapes
¼ x 1 kg/2 lb bag frozen chopped spinach, thawed
400 g/1 large can tomatoes, chopped
200 g/1 small can sweetcorn
½ tsp dried oregano
Salt and pepper
Grated Parmesan-style cheese, suitable for vegetarians

Anything
goes pasta

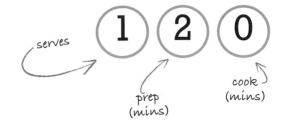

serves

1 2 0

prep (mins)

cook (mins)

There are no quantities or servings for this – it's too easy! Just use what you have to hand. The ingredients list is just a guide.

1 Cook the pasta in boiling, lightly salted water according to the packet directions. Drain, rinse with cold water and drain again.

2 Then add whatever combination of ingredients you have available.

3 Drizzle all over with oil, vinegar and some salt and pepper, add a pinch of dried oregano, toss and serve – delicious!

½–1 mug pasta shapes

FOR INSTANCE

Grated carrot

Chopped tomato

Chopped cucumber

Nuts

Raisins

Chopped apple or other fruit

Drained, canned vegetables or pulses

Sliced mushrooms

Onion rings

Oil

Vinegar

Salt and pepper

Pinch of dried oregano

Cheese- & egg-based dishes

Cheese and eggs are great forms of protein and, of course, they are very versatile. If you are vegan or a strict vegetarian, then obviously you will use non-dairy 'cheeses' and egg substitutes.

Some cheeses are expensive but there are always good deals to be had in supermarkets. Edam is cheaper than Cheddar but some varieties don't melt in the same way. Use it if you prefer.

Halloumi is great for grilling and is a wonderful substitute for meat.

Buy a strong cheese because you won't need as much of it to get a good flavour. So taste as you add it to a sauce, for instance, and if you've got a cheesy enough taste, save the rest for another meal. Many of the mild ones taste like soap and you could add them forever and never get a good result!

Cheese & vegetable soup

serves 4 · prep (mins) 10 · cook (mins) 20

For a tasty alternative, use crumbled blue cheese instead of Cheddar and leeks instead of onions – but make sure you wash them really well as they often contain lots of grit.

2 carrots, thinly sliced

2 onions, chopped

3 potatoes, thinly sliced

2 mugs boiling water

1 vegetable stock cube

½ tsp dried mixed herbs

¾ mug grated strong Cheddar cheese

1 mug milk

Salt and pepper

SERVE WITH

Crusty bread

1 Put the vegetables with the water, stock cube and herbs in a large saucepan. Bring to the boil, reduce the heat, part-cover and simmer for about 15 minutes until really soft.

2 Mash with a potato masher or use a hand blender if you have one.

3 Stir in the cheese, milk and salt and pepper to taste. Heat through, stirring, until the cheese melts.

4 Serve with lots of crusty bread.

Sandwiches in a blanket

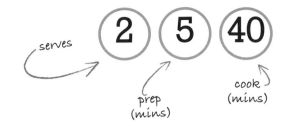

serves **2**

prep (mins) **5**

cook (mins) **40**

This is a surprisingly tasty, simple and economical dish, highly rated amongst the student population!

6 slices of <u>bread</u>, spread with a little <u>butter</u> or <u>margarine</u>

<u>Marmite</u>, or other <u>yeast extract</u>

1 mug grated <u>Cheddar cheese</u>

3 <u>tomatoes</u>, sliced

3 <u>eggs</u>

1 mug <u>milk</u>

<u>Salt and pepper</u>

½ tsp <u>dried mixed herbs</u>

SERVE WITH

<u>Green salad</u>

1 Preheat the oven to 190°C/375°F/gas 5/fan oven 170°C.

2 Make up sandwiches using the bread and butter or margarine, Marmite, three-quarters of the cheese and the tomatoes. Cut each round into four.

3 Arrange in the base of a shallow, ovenproof dish.

4 Beat together the eggs, milk, a little salt and pepper and the herbs and pour over the sandwiches. Sprinkle with the remaining cheese.

5 Bake in the oven for about 40 minutes until golden brown and set.

6 Serve with a crisp green salad.

Cauliflower cheese

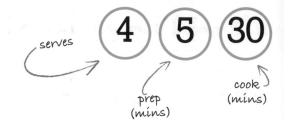

serves **4** prep (mins) **5** cook (mins) **30**

If you have a flameproof casserole dish, use that to cook the cauliflower then drain it in a colander; make the sauce in the same dish, return the cauliflower to it, then continue at step 4. Broccoli can be cooked the same way.

½ cauliflower, cut into florets
3 tbsp plain flour
1 mug milk
Knob of butter or margarine
½ tsp dried mixed herbs
½ tsp made mustard
Salt and pepper
¾ mug grated Cheddar cheese
2 handfuls of corn flakes or bran flakes, crushed
SERVE WITH
Canned or fresh tomatoes

1 Preheat the oven to 200°C/400°F/gas 6/fan oven 180°C or you can use the grill.

2 Cook the cauliflower in boiling, salted water until just tender – about 5 minutes, depending on the size of the florets. Drain in a colander.

3 Whisk the flour and milk together in the same saucepan until smooth. Add the butter or margarine. Bring to the boil and cook for 2 minutes, whisking all the time, until smooth and thickened.

4 Stir in the herbs, mustard and a little salt and pepper. Add three-quarters of the cheese. Fold in the cauliflower. Spoon into a flameproof dish.

5 Mix the remaining cheese with the crushed cereal and sprinkle over. Bake in the oven for 20 minutes or grill until golden and bubbling on top.

6 Serve with tomatoes.

Grilled Halloumi with peppers

serves (2) (5) (8)

prep (mins)

cook (mins)

You can buy value packs of peppers in many supermarkets. Alternatively, buy a pack of frozen roasted peppers and just heat half a packet through to serve with the Halloumi. You could use a couple of discs of goat's cheese instead.

2–3 tbsp olive or sunflower oil
4 peppers, preferably mixed colours, cut in thick slices
1 onion, sliced
Large pinch of dried basil
Salt and pepper
½ block Halloumi cheese, cut in 4 thick slices
SERVE WITH
Crusty bread

1 Heat half the oil in a large frying pan.

2 Add the peppers, onion and basil and fry, stirring, for about 5 minutes until softened but still with a little 'bite'. Season to taste.

3 Put the Halloumi on foil on the grill rack. Smear the remaining oil over both sides. Grill for a few minutes until turning golden in places and softening; no need to turn over.

4 Spoon the peppers on to plates, top with the cheese and serve with lots of crusty bread.

Curried cheese & corn grill

serves **2** prep (mins) **5** cook (mins) **10**

I like the extra kick of chilli powder but just use the curry powder if you prefer a milder flavour. If you have a flameproof casserole, use it instead of the saucepan and dish to save washing up.

1 Whisk the flour and milk together in a saucepan. Add the butter or margarine, bring to the boil and cook for 2 minutes, whisking all the time. Season to taste and stir in half the cheese.

2 Add the drained sweetcorn and pulses, the curry powder and chilli, if using. Heat through, stirring.

3 Preheat the grill. Spoon the mixture into a flameproof dish. Sprinkle with the remaining cheese and place under the hot grill until golden and bubbling

4 Serve hot with broccoli and toast.

3 tbsp plain flour

1 mug milk

Knob of butter or margarine

Salt and pepper

¾ mug grated Cheddar cheese

200 g/1 small can sweetcorn, drained

425 g/1 large can mixed pulses, drained

1 tsp curry powder or paste

¼ tsp chilli powder (optional)

SERVE WITH

Broccoli and toast

Greek-style feta salad

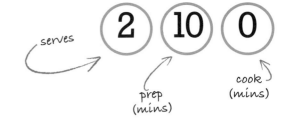

serves **2**
prep (mins) **10**
cook (mins) **0**

This is delicious as a meal on its own or great in a smaller quantity to accompany stuffed peppers, fried sliced aubergines or an omelette. Quick and delicious.

¼–½ small crisp <u>lettuce</u>, shredded

2 <u>tomatoes</u>, cut into chunks

5 cm piece of <u>cucumber</u>, cut into chunks

1 small <u>onion</u>, sliced and separated into rings

½ block <u>feta cheese</u>, cubed or crumbled

A few <u>olives</u> (optional)

2 tbsp <u>pine nuts</u> (optional)

A little <u>oil</u>

A little <u>vinegar</u>

<u>Salt and pepper</u>

¼–½ tsp <u>dried mixed herbs</u> or <u>oregano</u>

SERVE WITH

Warm <u>pitta bread</u>

1 Put the lettuce in 2 shallow bowls. Top with the tomatoes, cucumber, onion and then the cheese. Scatter the olives and pine nuts (if using) over the top.

2 Drizzle with a little oil and vinegar, sprinkle very lightly with salt and add lots of pepper. Sprinkle with the herbs.

3 Serve with lots of warm pitta bread.

Cheese & pineapple **salad**

serves **2**

prep (mins) **3**

cook (mins) **0**

This is a good way to use up any pineapple left over from another recipe. Or, if you are left with pineapple from this, eat it for dessert or on your cereal. It goes well with the nuts and cheese.

1 Mix the pineapple, cheese, walnuts, chives and pepper.

2 Put some lettuce in a bowl and top with the salad.

3 Serve with crackers or bread

1 canned pineapple ring, chopped

1 small carton cottage cheese

1 tbsp chopped walnuts

1 tsp dried chives

Pepper

A few lettuce leaves

Paprika

TO SERVE

Crackers or bread

Cheese & tomato **pan pizza**

serves **1** prep (mins) **15** cook (mins) **10**

Add other toppings of your choice before adding the cheese, if you like, such as a few sliced mushrooms, a handful of sweetcorn, a few sliced olives or some chopped peppers (or a few thawed frozen roasted ones).

1 mug <u>self-raising flour</u>
A pinch of <u>salt</u>
3 tbsp <u>sunflower</u> or <u>olive oil</u>
About 4 tbsp <u>cold water</u>
225 g/1 small can <u>chopped tomatoes</u>, drained
¼ tsp <u>dried oregano</u>
Handful of grated <u>Cheddar</u>, <u>Edam</u> or <u>Mozzarella cheese</u>
SERVE WITH
<u>Mixed salad</u>

1 Mix the flour and salt in a bowl. Add 2 tbsp of the oil and mix with cold water, a little at a time, to form a soft but not sticky dough (you may need slightly more or less depending on the flour).

2 Squeeze it together gently to form a ball, then put it on a lightly floured surface and roll out to a round the size of a medium frying pan, using a rolling pin or a clean bottle. Alternatively you can pat it out with your hand.

3 Heat the remaining oil in the frying pan and add the base. Cook for 3 minutes until golden brown underneath.

4 Turn over and top with the tomatoes, oregano and cheese. Cover with a lid or foil and cook over a fairly gentle heat for about 5 minutes until the cheese has melted. If liked, put the pan under a preheated grill to brown the top.

almost finished

5 Serve with lots of salad.

Cottage cheese omelette wedges

serves **2** prep (mins) **3** cook (mins) **6**

Cottage cheese is an often forgotten ingredient that is low in fat and high in protein. You can use one flavoured with chives or peppers for added flavour, or try adding a grated carrot or courgette instead of the sliced mushrooms.

2 eggs, beaten
200 g/1 small carton cottage cheese
5 tbsp milk
Salt and pepper
4 mushrooms, sliced
1 small onion, chopped
Pinch of dried mixed herbs
Knob of butter or margarine
SERVE WITH
Salad roll or sandwich

1 Mix all the ingredients except the butter or margarine in a bowl. Preheat the grill.

2 Heat a frying pan with the knob of butter or margarine. When sizzling, swirl round to coat the base.

3 Add the omelette mixture and cook over a moderate heat, lifting and stirring until almost set and golden brown underneath.

4 Pop the pan under the grill for a few minutes to brown the top (be careful of the handle),

5 Serve cut into wedges, with a salad roll or sandwich.

Rolled green bean omelette

serves **4** prep (mins) **3** cook (mins) **10**

If you're feeling decadent, canned asparagus spears taste great served like this or, for a more Asian flavour, add drained, canned or fresh bean sprouts instead and sprinkle with soy sauce before rolling up.

4 eggs
4 tbsp cold water
Salt and pepper
1 tsp dried mixed herbs
Butter or margarine
300 g/1 medium can whole
green beans, drained
SERVE WITH
Crusty bread and chunky salad
pieces

1 Beat one of the eggs in a bowl with 1 tbsp of water, a little salt and pepper and $\frac{1}{4}$ tsp herbs.

2 Heat a little butter or margarine in a frying pan. Pour in the egg and fry, lifting the edge and letting uncooked egg run underneath until set. Transfer to a plate and leave to cool while you make 3 more omelettes in the same way.

3 Divide the beans between the omelettes and roll them up.

4 Serve with crusty bread and chunky salad pieces that can be eaten with your fingers.

Eggy pizza baguette

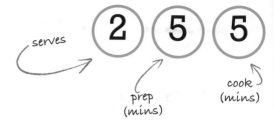

serves **2**

prep (mins) **5**

cook (mins) **5**

Eggs have had a bad press in recent years but they are a good, nutritious food – as well as being quick and easy to cook. Buy eggs with the Lion mark, keep them in the fridge and watch the use-by date.

1 small <u>French baguette</u>
<u>Butter</u> or <u>margarine</u>
2 <u>eggs</u>
2 tbsp <u>water</u>
¼ tsp <u>dried mixed herbs</u> or <u>oregano</u>
Handful of grated Cheddar cheese
1 tomato, sliced
<u>Salt and pepper</u>
TO SERVE
<u>Salad</u>

1 Warm the baguette either in the oven or under the grill, turning frequently. Cut a slit along the length and spread with butter or margarine.

2 Meanwhile, break the eggs in a bowl. Add the water, herbs and some salt and pepper. Beat well with a whisk or fork. Stir in the cheese.

3 Heat a frying pan and add a knob of butter or margarine. When sizzling, pour in the egg mixture. Lift and stir the mixture with a fish slice or spatula for a few minutes until almost set, but still creamy on top.

4 Lay two tomato slices on top. Cover with foil, a lid or a plate. Cook gently until the tomato softens and the omelette is set.

5 Slide the omelette out on to a plate and roll up. Lay it in the French stick and cut in half.

Eggs with creamed leeks

Leeks have a lovely mild onion flavour that goes really well with eggs. It's important to wash them well as they tend to be gritty. Slit them almost in half not quite to the root end and wash between the layers with cold running water.

125 g butter or margarine

2 large leeks, sliced

1 mug boiling water

1 vegetable stock cube

3 tbsp dried milk powder or double cream

3 tbsp plain flour

4 tbsp water

Salt and pepper

4 eggs

SERVE WITH

Toast

1 Melt the butter or margarine in a saucepan. Add the leeks and cook, stirring, for 2 minutes.

2 Stir in the boiling water and stock cube, bring to the boil, reduce the heat, part-cover and simmer for 10 minutes or until the leeks are really tender.

3 Blend the milk powder, flour and water together to a smooth cream. Stir into the leeks and cook, stirring, for 2 minutes until thickened and smooth. Season to taste.

4 Meanwhile, hard-boil the eggs (see page 15). Drain and plunge quickly into cold water. Shell and cut into halves.

5 Put the eggs into 2 warm shallow bowls and spoon the leek sauce over the top.

6 Serve with lots of toast.

Stuffed pancakes

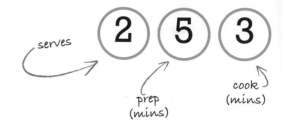

Always use a non-stick frying pan and don't worry if the first pancake doesn't go too well. The pan gets 'seasoned' as it's used and the second one will cook a treat! Serve with any of the savoury fillings, suggested opposite, or use for dessert.

8 tbsp <u>plain four</u>
Pinch of <u>salt</u>
1 <u>egg</u>
½ mug <u>milk</u> and <u>water</u> mixed
<u>Oil</u> for frying

1 Put the flour and salt in a bowl. Break in the egg (break into a cup first if you're not a dab hand at it).

2 Add half the milk and water and beat with a whisk until smooth. Stir in the remaining milk and water. The mixture should be the consistency of thin cream. Add a dash more milk if necessary.

3 Heat a very little oil in a frying pan until smoking. Pour off the excess into a cup to use for the next pancake, leaving the pan thinly coated with oil. Add about a ladle-full (3 tbsp) of batter – or enough to form a thin coat over the base of the pan when quickly tilted round. You have to work fast!

4 Cook over a moderate heat until the top of the pancake is set and dry. Toss, or flip over with a fish slice, and cook the other side briefly, then slide on to a plate over a pan of simmering water to keep it warm while cooking the remainder.

5 To serve, spread a little chosen filling on to each pancake, roll up and eat. If you want to be flash, fill the pancakes, pack into a shallow ovenproof dish, dot with a little butter or margarine, sprinkle with some grated cheese and heat through in a preheated oven at 190°C/375°F/gas 5/fan oven 170°C for about 20 minutes until piping hot and the top is sizzling.

almost finished

Suggested
speedy fillings

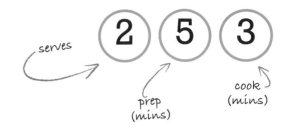

serves 2 · prep (mins) 5 · cook (mins) 3

If eating alone, 2 pancakes will keep in the fridge, wrapped in foil or clingfilm, for up to 3 days.

The quantity of batter on page 152 makes 4 pancakes, which will serve 2 people.
Take a look in the cupboard or fridge and use what you've got to fill your pancakes. Sweet or savoury fillings work equally well, depending on your mood.

- **Ratatouille and cheese:** Heat a can of ratatouille, spread over the pancakes and sprinkle with grated cheese (try Mozzarella) before rolling

- **Baked bean and cheese:** Heat a can of baked beans, spread over the pancakes, sprinkle with grated cheese and roll up. Heat through if you like.

- **Spinach and cottage cheese:** Cook 4 handfuls of frozen spinach according to the packet directions. Drain off any excess water. Stir in a small carton of cottage cheese, heat through and season well, adding a little grated nutmeg if liked. Spread on the pancakes and roll up.

- **French cheese and tomato:** Slice a small Camembert cheese, lay the slices on a flat pancake add some slices of tomato and top with a second pancake. Heat through in the oven before serving.

- **Egg and cheese:** Top each pancake with some thin slices of cheese and a poached or fried egg in the centre. Fold over the edges of the pancake so the egg is still visible before serving.

- **Chilli bean pancakes:** Mash a drained can of red kidney beans with a dash of tomato ketchup and chilli powder to taste. Add a little garlic from a jar or tube if you like. Moisten, if necessary, with water. Spread the pancakes with the mixture. Roll up, sprinkle with grated cheese and heat through in the oven before serving.

Tortilla

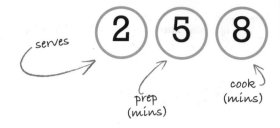

This can be made with leftover cooked potato. Tortilla is delicious served hot or cold with salad. It is the original Spanish omelette but you could add some sliced peppers or courgettes to the mixture for added colour and flavour.

1 large potato, thinly sliced

1 small onion, chopped

1 tbsp oil

Salt and pepper

4 eggs, beaten

1 Put the potato and onion with the oil in a frying pan and fry for 4 minutes, stirring, until the potato and onions are really soft.

2 Add a little seasoning and the eggs. Cook gently, lifting and stirring at first, until the egg has almost set.

3 Place under a hot grill to brown and set the top.

4 Serve cut into wedges.

Mock cheese soufflé

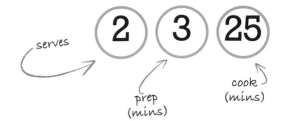

serves **2**

prep (mins) **3**

cook (mins) **25**

This tastes as good as a cheese soufflé but is more substantial and less effort. You can stand the open can of tomatoes on the oven shelf (on foil to catch drips) to heat up while it cooks, or serve it with tomato salad or baked beans.

Large knob of <u>butter</u> or <u>margarine</u>
1 <u>egg</u>, separated (page 20)
½ mug <u>milk</u>
2 thick slices of <u>bread</u>, crusts removed
½ mug grated <u>Cheddar cheese</u>
<u>Salt and pepper</u>
SERVE WITH
<u>Canned tomatoes</u>

1 Preheat the oven to 200°C/400°F/gas 6/fan oven 180°C. Grease an ovenproof dish well with the butter or margarine.

2 Beat the egg yolk with the milk in the greased dish and crumble in the bread. Add the cheese and a little salt and pepper. Leave to stand for 15 minutes.

3 Whisk the egg white until stiff in a clean bowl with a metal whisk and gently fold into the mixture with a metal spoon, using a figure-of-eight motion.

4 Cook in the oven for about 25 minutes until risen and golden.

5 Serve immediately with canned tomatoes.

Egg & potato salad

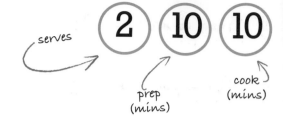

serves — 2 10 10
prep (mins) cook (mins)

I like adding some olives and a few fresh torn basil leaves to this but it's only a suggestion as it's perfectly fine on its own. You could add a small can of sweetcorn too, if you like.

6–8 new potatoes, scrubbed and cut into bite-sized pieces
2 eggs, scrubbed under the cold tap
1 tbsp mayonnaise
1 tsp vinegar
1 tsp dried mint or chives
Salt and pepper
Lettuce leaves
2 tomatoes, sliced

1 Put the potatoes and eggs (in their shells) in a saucepan of lightly salted water. Bring to the boil and boil until the potatoes are tender. Take the eggs out after 10 minutes (whether or not the potatoes are cooked) and plunge into cold water. Drain the potatoes when cooked and leave to cool.

2 Mix the mayonnaise, vinegar, herbs and a little salt and pepper together. Add the potatoes.

3 Shell the eggs and roughly chop. Add to the bowl and mix together gently but thoroughly. Preferably chill for several hours to allow the flavours to develop.

4 Spoon on to lettuce leaves and add the slices of tomato.

Onion & cheese frittata

serves **2** prep **10** (mins) cook **14** (mins)

I like this made with Pecorino cheese but that's a bit more expensive than other options, so just choose a good strong cheese if you are strapped for cash.

2 small _onions_, thinly sliced

1 tbsp _oil_

2 _eggs_

50 g strong _cheese_, grated

Pinch of _dried mixed herbs_

Salt and pepper

1 Fry the onions in the oil in a small frying pan over medium heat for 5 minutes until soft.

2 Beat the eggs in a bowl until frothy, then stir in the cheese, herbs, salt and pepper.

3 Pour the egg mixture into the pan and cook for 4–5 minutes until set on top.

4 Turn the frittata carefully and cook for 4 minutes more. It should be firm and lightly browned on both sides.

Energy
boosters

Make a batch of any of the following before you have to get stuck into revising or serious exam schedules. Then you'll have something highly comforting and packed with goodness to give you extra energy any time of the day or night. They're ideal to nibble when you're feeling low or shattered or you've skipped a meal (like breakfast when you've overslept from all that studying ... or whatever!). None of them takes long to make and they are all far cheaper than buying equivalent bars in the supermarket or health food shop.

Chocolate
walnut brownies

makes **15** **10** **35**

If you don't like nuts, leave them out or add a couple of large handfuls of raisins to the mixture. The coffee enhances the chocolate flavour but you can omit that too if you prefer.

1 Preheat the oven to 180°C/350°F/gas 4/fan oven 160°C.

2 Melt the butter or margarine, chocolate chips, sugar and coffee in a saucepan, stirring.

3 Remove from the heat and stir in the remaining ingredients.

4 Turn into a greased 18 x 28 cm baking tin. Bake in the oven for 35 minutes until the mixture springs back when lightly pressed.

5 Cool in the tin, then cut into squares and store in an airtight container.

⅓ x 250g tub <u>butter</u> or <u>margarine</u>
½ x small packet <u>chocolate chips</u>
¾ mug <u>sugar</u>
½ tsp <u>instant coffee granules</u>
2 <u>eggs</u>, beaten
¼ x 200 g packet <u>walnut pieces</u>, chopped
½ mug <u>plain</u> or <u>wholemeal flour</u>
¼ tsp <u>baking powder</u>
¼ tsp <u>salt</u>

Peanut honey bites

makes **12** **10** **0**

prep (mins)

cook (mins)

These biscuits make a nutritious snack when serious study is at hand. Look out for packets of broken biscuits or own-brands, they're really inexpensive and ideal for this recipe.

1 Melt the butter or margarine with the honey and bring to the boil. Remove from the heat.

2 Stir in the remaining ingredients and mix well.

3 Press into a greased 18 cm square baking tin or similar sized container and chill until set. Cut into squares and store in airtight tin.

½ x 250 g tub <u>butter</u> or <u>margarine</u>
3 tbsp <u>thick honey</u>
⅔ x 300 g packet of <u>plain biscuits</u>, roughly crushed
1 tsp grated <u>lemon rind</u> (optional.)
3 tbsp <u>crunchy peanut butter</u>

Mum's
flapjacks

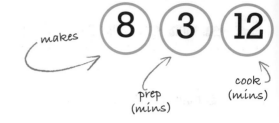

makes **8**

prep (mins) **3**

cook (mins) **12**

Easy and delicious – and, of course, oats are good for you. When you want a real taste of home, you can't beat a good flapjack. Plus they transport well so you can take one with you for a mid-morning snack.

⅓ x 250 g tub <u>butter</u> or <u>margarine</u>

2 tbsp <u>brown sugar</u>

2 tbsp <u>golden syrup</u>

1½ mugs <u>porridge oats</u>

⅓ mug <u>plain flour</u>

1 Preheat the oven to 190°C/375°F/gas 5/fan oven 170°C and grease an 18 cm square baking tin.

2 Melt the butter, sugar and syrup in a pan.

3 Stir in the remaining ingredients and mix well.

4 Cook in the oven for about 12 minutes until golden.

5 Leave to cool for 5 minutes, then mark into portions. Leave to cool completely before removing from the tin.

6 Store in an airtight container.

Banana sultana flapjacks

makes 16 — prep (mins) 8 — cook (mins) 30

This recipe was hailed by a medical student friend of mine and her flat-mates as the food they lived on most! It's cheap, nutritious and delicious when you're studying – or when you're just chilling.

⅓ x 250 g tub butter or margarine, softened
½ mug light brown (preferably) sugar
1 tbsp golden syrup or honey
1 large, ripe banana, mashed
2 handfuls of sultanas or raisins
2½ mugs porridge oats

1 Preheat the oven to 180°C/350°F/gas 4/fan oven 160°C.

2 Put the butter or margarine, sugar and syrup or honey in a bowl and beat with a wooden spoon until smooth and fluffy.

3 Stir in the remaining ingredients and press into a greased 18 x 28 cm baking tin.

4 Bake in the oven for about 30 minutes or until golden brown.

5 Leave to cool for 10 minutes then mark into fingers with the back of a knife. Leave until completely cold before cutting up. Store in an airtight tin.

Spiced
popcorn

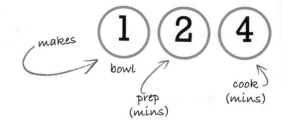

The lid is essential. Did you know, this is what the microwave was invented for? Instead of frying, microwave in 30-second bursts in a see-through covered bowl so you can tell when it has puffed up but stopped popping.

2 tbsp <u>oil</u>

½ mug <u>popping corn</u>

1 tsp <u>garam masala</u>, <u>Chinese five-spices</u>, <u>ground cumin</u>, or <u>cajun spices</u>

A pinch of <u>chilli powder</u> (optional)

<u>Salt</u>

1   Heat the oil in a large pan with a lid.

2   Add the corn, put on the lid and cook over a moderate heat. The corn will start to pop. Shake the pan occasionally, holding on to the lid (but don't take it off!) until the popping stops.

3   Remove the lid, sprinkle on the spices and a little salt. Tip into a large bowl and toss again to mix in the flavouring.

Sweet butter popcorn

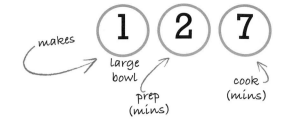

makes

1 large bowl

2 prep (mins)

7 cook (mins)

The sweet option is not quite as good for you so lay off this one if you nibble your way through your revision. This is the 'treat' option! Remember, the lid is essential, and the microwave is an option (see page 164).

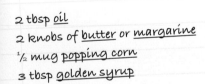

2 tbsp oil
2 knobs of butter or margarine
½ mug popping corn
3 tbsp golden syrup

1. Heat the oil and a knob of butter or margarine in a large pan with a lid.

2. Add the corn, put on the lid and cook over a moderate heat. The corn will start to pop. Shake the pan occasionally, holding on to the lid (but don't take it off!) until the popping stops.

3. Remove the lid and add the rest of the butter or margarine and the syrup. Cook, stirring and tossing, for about 3 minutes until all the corn is coated in the buttery syrup. Take care not to let it burn.

4. Tip into a large bowl and leave to cool.

Chewy fruit & coconut bars

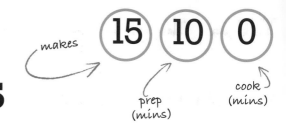

makes **15** **10** **0**

prep (mins) cook (mins)

These bars are great energy boosters during cramming sessions. You can substitute any other dried fruit – such as dates, prunes or raisins – for the apricots if you prefer.

175 g/1 small can <u>evaporated milk</u>
4 tsp <u>thick honey</u>
3 tbsp <u>apple</u> or <u>orange juice</u>
¼ x 250 g tub <u>butter</u> or <u>margarine</u>
¼ mug <u>light brown</u> (preferably) <u>sugar</u>
2 large handfuls of <u>sultanas</u>
1 mug ready-to-eat <u>dried apricots</u>, chopped
½ mug <u>desiccated coconut</u>
2 mugs <u>porridge oats</u>

1 Heat the evaporated milk with the honey, juice, butter or margarine and sugar until just melted. Remove from the heat.

2 Add the remaining ingredients and mix well. Press into a greased 28 x 18 cm baking tin or similar sized container.

3 Wrap in clingfilm or put in a clean plastic carrier bag and chill overnight to allow the flavours to develop before cutting into bars.

4 Store in an airtight container in the fridge.

No-bake
crunch bars

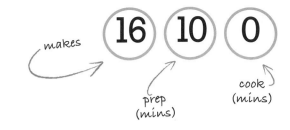

makes **16**

prep (mins) **10**

cook (mins) **0**

Chocolate is comfort food at its best. If you buy a good quality one with high cocoa solids, it's actually good for you (in small portions) as it is high in antioxidants and stimulates endorphins in your brain to make you feel good.

⅔ x 250 g tub <u>butter</u> or <u>margarine</u>
¼ mug <u>light brown</u> (preferably) <u>sugar</u>
2 tbsp <u>golden syrup</u>
3 tbsp <u>cocoa powder</u>
½ mug <u>raisins</u>
3 mugs <u>oat crunch-type cereal</u>
200 g bar <u>plain chocolate</u>

1 Oil and line the base of an 18 x 28 cm baking tin with baking parchment, greaseproof paper or the inside wrapper from a cereal packet.

2 Melt the butter or margarine, sugar and syrup and cocoa in a large saucepan. Remove from the heat. Stir in the raisins and cereal until well blended. Press into the tin.

3 Melt the chocolate in a pan over hot water and spread over the top, right into the corners.

4 Chill until set, cut into fingers and store in an airtight tin.

Desserts

Most students live off yoghurts or fresh fruit for 'afters' which is a great idea. But every now and then you might hanker after a real pud – something sweet and luscious but still good for you. Here are some really simple ideas which taste terrific and are ideal for filling up on – especially when you have people round to share them with. None of them is exactly rocket science but the attraction is their simplicity.

Ice cream & chocolate sauces

serves **4**

prep (mins) **5**

cook (mins) **5**

Ice cream is a great standby. You can buy all kinds of fruit or toffee sauces, sprinkle on some nuts, chopped fruit or drizzle with honey – but nothing beats a chocolate or caramel option, so here are two to try.

8 scoops of _ice cream_

FOR THE CARAMEL SAUCE

2 _Mars bars_, chopped

4 tbsp _milk_

Knob of _butter_ or _margarine_

FOR THE CHOCOLATE SAUCE

1 x 200 g bar _plain chocolate_, broken into pieces

4 tbsp _butter_ or _margarine_

3 tbsp _brown_ or _caster sugar_

2 tbsp _golden syrup_

Scant mug _milk_

1 To make the caramel sauce, melt the Mars bars, milk and butter gently in a pan, stirring occasionally until melted. Add a little more milk, if liked.

2 To make the chocolate sauce, set a heatproof bowl on top of a pan of gently simmering water. Add the chocolate and butter or margarine and stir until melted.

3 Add the sugar and syrup, stirring until dissolved.

4 Pour in the milk and stir gently until the mixture thickens.

5 To serve, pour the hot sauce over the ice cream in bowls and serve straight away.

Bread pudding

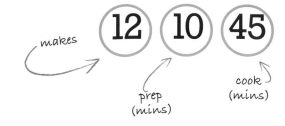

This is a great way to use up a stale loaf of bread and it will keep well in a sealed container in the fridge for a few days. It's great for snacking on late at night too! White sugar is fine if you don't have brown.

1 mug milk
Pinch of salt
¼ x 250 g tub butter or margarine
8 slices of bread, cubed
2 eggs, beaten
1 mug mixed dried fruit
3 tbsp light brown sugar
1 tsp mixed spice or cinnamon
A little caster sugar for dusting

1 Put the milk, salt and butter or margarine in a large saucepan and bring to the boil. Remove from the heat.

2 Add the bread and leave to stand for 15 minutes.

3 Preheat the oven to 180°C/350°F/gas 4/fan oven 160°C.

4 Add the remaining ingredients except the caster sugar for dusting and mix well. Turn into a greased baking tin and bake in the oven for about 45 minutes until lightly browned and set.

5 Sprinkle with caster sugar and serve hot or cold, cut into squares.

Pineapple
loaf

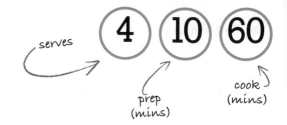

This is, basically, a pineapple cake that is just as good for snacks as for dessert. It is really good with lashings of custard though! You can use a small can of crushed pineapple, well drained, instead of chopping the canned rings.

3 mugs <u>plain flour</u>

1 tbsp <u>baking powder</u>

½ tsp <u>bicarbonate of soda</u>

½ mug <u>light brown sugar</u>

⅔ x 250g tub <u>butter</u> or <u>margarine</u>, softened

3 <u>eggs</u>, beaten

2 tbsp <u>milk</u>

1 tsp <u>ground cinnamon</u>

2 tbsp <u>honey</u>

225 g/1 small can <u>pineapple rings</u>, drained, the fruit chopped and the juice reserved

1 Preheat the oven to 180°C/350°F/gas 4/fan oven 160°C.

2 Put all the ingredients in a large bowl and beat together well with a wooden spoon until soft, adding a little extra milk, if necessary, so the mixture will drop in a soft dollop off the spoon.

3 Turn into a greased large loaf tin or a baking dish and bake on a low shelf in the oven for about 1 hour or until firm to the touch.

4 Leave to cool for a few minutes. Loosen the edges and turn out.

5 Serve warm or cold with the reserved juice, if liked.

Sweet pancakes

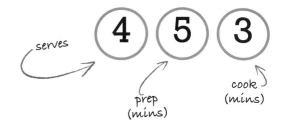

serves 4
prep (mins) 5
cook (mins) 3

Pancakes are the ultimate comfort food. And they are so easy to make, you shouldn't resort to buying packets of ready-made. Hot from the pan, they are delicious!

1 Make the pancakes according to the directions on page 152.

2 Either sprinkle with sugar and lemon juice or spread with a little warm jam or honey.

3 Roll up and serve.

1 quantity of pancake mix (see Stuffed pancakes page 152)
Caster sugar and lemon juice
OR any flavour jam or honey, warmed

Chocolate
nut crêpes

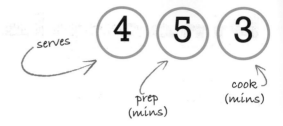

You can fill pancakes with sweet or savoury mixes – this is one of my daughter's favourite sweet versions, making good use of that old favourite, chocolate spread.

1   Make up the pancakes according to the directions on page 152.

2   Spread each with a little chocolate hazelnut spread, sprinkle with a few nuts and roll up.

3   Serve with a dollop of crème fraîche or yoghurt or a spoonful of ice cream on top of each portion.

1 quantity of pancake mix (see Stuffed pancakes page 152)

Chocolate hazelnut spread

Handful of chopped mixed nuts

A little crème fraîche, thick plain yoghurt or ice cream

Pineapple pudding

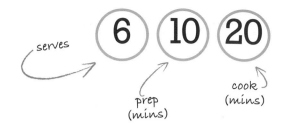

serves **6** **10** **20**

prep (mins)

cook (mins)

This pudding is just as good cold as hot. You can use canned peaches instead of pineapple or try pears and use a chocolate sponge cake mix. It's great to keep in the fridge to cut-and-come-again to over a few days.

Knob of butter or margarine
2 tbsp light brown sugar or golden syrup
225 g/1 small can pineapple rings, drained, reserving the juice
Glacé cherries, halved or a few sultanas
1 packet sponge cake mix
Egg and water according to the packet directions

1 Preheat the oven to 190°C/375°F/gas 5/fan oven 170°C and liberally grease a 20 cm round sandwich tin or other shallow ovenproof dish with the butter or margarine.

2 Sprinkle the sugar over the base, then top with the pineapple rings.

3 Place a halved glacé cherry, cut-side up, in the centre of each ring, or a few sultanas or raisins here and in the gaps around.

4 Make up the sponge mixture according to the packet directions. Spoon over the fruit.

5 Bake in the oven for 20 minutes until risen and the centre springs back when lightly pressed.

6 Leave to cool slightly in the tin, then loosen the edges with a round-bladed knife and turn out on to a serving plate. Serve with the juice.

Pear batter bake

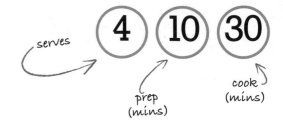

serves **4**

prep (mins) **10**

cook (mins) **30**

Cans or boxes of custard are brilliant. Serve cold, or warm gently in a microwave or pan. This works just as well with other fruit, so try it with whatever you like.

1 quantity of <u>pancake mix</u> (see Stuffed pancakes page 152)
410 g/1 large can <u>pears</u>, drained and diced, reserving the juice
Handful of <u>flaked almonds</u> (optional)
<u>Caster sugar</u>
SERVE WITH
<u>Custard</u>

1 Preheat the oven to 200°C/400°F/gas 6/fan oven 180°C.

2 Spread out the pears in the base of a greased, shallow, ovenproof dish.

3 Make up the batter mix and pour over the pears. Sprinkle with nuts, if using.

4 Bake in the oven for about 30 minutes until set and golden.

5 Dust with caster sugar before serving with custard.

No-effort
fruit crumble

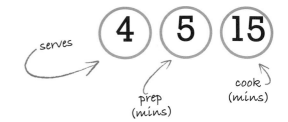

serves **4**
prep (mins) **5**
cook (mins) **15**

This is a really nutritious dessert, great to put in the oven when you're using it for a main course anyway. You can, of course, use any canned fruit you like – rhubarb is good, but so are apple, peaches or apricots.

410 g/1 large can <u>fruit</u>, drained, reserving the juice

¼ x 250 g tub <u>butter</u> or <u>margarine</u>

2 <u>Weetabix</u>

1 tbsp <u>light brown</u> (preferably) <u>sugar</u>

½ tsp <u>ground ginger</u>, <u>cinnamon</u> or <u>mixed spice</u>

SERVE WITH

<u>Cream</u> or <u>custard</u>

1 Preheat the oven to 190°C/375°F/gas 5/fan oven 170°C.

2 Put the fruit in an ovenproof dish.

3 Melt the margarine in a saucepan.

4 Remove from the heat and crumble in the Weetabix. Stir in the sugar and spice.

5 Sprinkle the topping over the fruit, pressing down lightly.

almost finished

6 Bake in the oven for about 15 minutes until crisp. Serve warm with cream or custard.

Instant
chocolate mousse

serves **4**

prep (mins) **5**

cook (mins) **0**

This is so easy but tastes fantastic. The only effort is whipping the cream with a hand whisk if you don't have an electric one. For a special occasion, add a tablespoon of spirit such as vodka, rum or whisky with the chocolate.

284 ml carton <u>double</u> or <u>whipping cream</u>
2 heaped tbsp <u>chocolate spread</u>
(or chocolate and hazelnut)
A little <u>chocolate</u>, grated
(optional)

1 Whip the cream in a large bowl with a metal whisk until it stands in soft peaks. Spoon off about a third and reserve.

2 Add the chocolate spread to the remainder and whisk gently until thoroughly combined. Spoon into glasses or dishes and top with the reserved cream. If liked, grate a little chocolate over the surface to decorate.

3 Chill for 1–2 hours to firm up a bit.

Chunky fruit fool

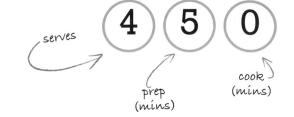

serves **4**

prep (mins) **5**

cook (mins) **0**

This is really a flash way of serving fruit and custard but it somehow tastes much better like this! If eating alone, the remaining fool will keep in the fridge to eat over the next few days.

1 Mash the fruit well with a fork.

2 Stir in the custard, then fold in the yoghurt.

3 Spoon into glasses.

4 Serve chilled with the juice poured over at the last minute.

410 g/1 large can <u>apricots</u> (or other fruit) in natural juice, drained, reserving the juice
400 g/1 large can <u>custard</u>
1 small carton thick plain <u>Greek-style yoghurt</u>

Little orange trifle

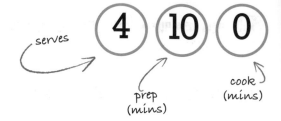

serves **4**

prep (mins) **10**

cook (mins) **0**

Broken mandarin segments are much cheaper than the whole ones and taste just as good in this simple old favourite, although obviously the whole ones are fine too!

1 jam <u>Swiss roll</u>, sliced
300 g/1 small can <u>broken mandarin segments</u>
1 packet <u>orange-flavoured vegetarian jelly</u>
400 g/1 large can <u>custard</u>, chilled
A small piece of <u>plain chocolate</u>

1 Put the Swiss roll slices in the base of a serving dish.

2 Drain the mandarin pieces, reserving the juice. Scatter the fruit over the Swiss roll.

3 Make up the jelly using the juice instead of some of the water. Cool slightly, then pour over the sponge and fruit and chill until set.

4 Spoon the custard over and grate the chocolate over the top before serving.

Raspberry
layer dessert

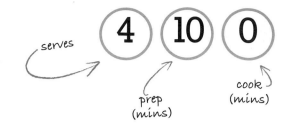

serves **4**   prep (mins) **10**   cook (mins) **0**

You can use quark instead of ordinary soft white cheese if you prefer. It's a really simple dessert that's just delicious with strawberries and strawberry jelly for a change.

1 Make up the raspberries and their juice to 2½ mugs with water. Use a little to dissolve the jelly, then stir in the remainder.

2 Whisk in the cheese, then pour into a serving dish. The mixture will separate as it cools. Chill for a few hours, or overnight, until set.

300 g/1 small can raspberries
1 packet raspberry-flavoured vegetarian jelly
½ small carton low-fat soft white cheese

Bananas with hot lemon sauce

serves **2**   prep (mins) **5**   cook (mins) **3**

This hot lemon sauce is great just spooned over ice cream or with pancakes (see page 152). You could serve it more like a banana split with the banana halved lengthways, scoops of ice cream in the middle and the sauce spooned over.

1 Put the margarine, sugar and lemon juice in a small pan. Heat gently, stirring until well blended and the sugar has melted, if using. Simmer for 1 minute.

2 Divide the yoghurt or ice cream between 2 glasses. Top with sliced bananas.

3 Spoon the sauce over and serve straight away.

Large knob of <u>butter</u> or <u>margarine</u>
3 tbsp <u>light brown sugar</u> or <u>honey</u>
1 tbsp <u>lemon juice</u>
1 small carton <u>plain yoghurt</u>
OR 4 spoonfuls <u>ice cream</u>
2 <u>bananas</u>, sliced

Banana split

This old favourite is so quick and easy to make – with the added bonus that you have here the quickest chocolate sauce that you can create in minutes to pour over just about anything. The ultimate comfort food.

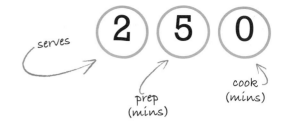

serves **2**

prep (mins) **5**

cook (mins) **0**

2 bananas, split lengthways
4 scoops vanilla ice cream
2 large spoonfuls chocolate spread
A little milk or water
A few chopped nuts (optional)

1 Put the bananas and ice cream in serving dishes.

2 Put the chocolate spread in a pan and add a splash of milk or water. Heat gently, stirring all the time until smooth and runny. Add a little more milk or water, if necessary, to give a pouring consistency.

3 Pour over the bananas and ice cream and serve sprinkled with a few chopped nuts, if you like.

Banoffee
brûlée

 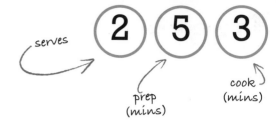
You could make other brûlées the same way using different fruits in season, such as sliced strawberries, plums or nectarines with the matching fruit yoghurt or vanilla yoghurt and the sugar over the top.

2 bananas
1 small carton toffee yoghurt
2-3 tbsp light brown sugar

1 Preheat the grill.

2 Slice the bananas and place in 2 individual flameproof dishes.

3 Spoon the yoghurt over.

4 Sprinkle liberally with the sugar to cover the tops completely.

5 Remove the grill rack and place the dishes in the pan. Grill until the sugar melts and bubbles.

6 Serve straight away.

Instant cheesecakes

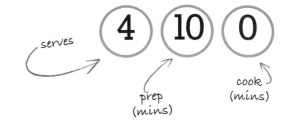

serves 4
prep (mins) 10
cook (mins) 0

This tastes really good but is very easy to make and much better than commercial cheesecakes that tend to taste very synthetic. Add a little finely grated lemon zest to the mixture if you have one to hand.

1 Put the slices of cake into 4 serving dishes.

2 Mash the fruits, reserving 4 whole ones (or halved strawberries) for decoration.

3 Stir in the cheese and sugar and mix well.

4 Pile on the cake and top each with a whole berry. Chill until ready to serve.

4 slices of slab sponge cake
4 handfuls of soft fruits in season (e.g. strawberries, raspberries or blackberries)
1 x 200g carton low-fat soft cheese
1 tbsp caster (superfine) sugar

Banana ginger layer **cake**

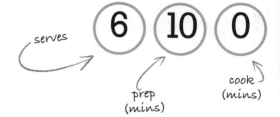

serves **6**

prep (mins) **10**

cook (mins) **0**

Bananas and ginger go really well. If you don't want to be bothered to make up the cake, cut slices of the ginger cake, top with the mashed bananas and lemon, then add a dollop of crème fraîche and some grated chocolate.

1. Cut the cake lengthways into 3 slices.

2. Mash the bananas with the lemon juice and use to sandwich the layers back together again.

3. Gently spread the crème fraîche over the top and grate a little chocolate over.

4. Chill well before serving, cut into slices (the tricky bit!).

1 slab Jamaican ginger cake

2 bananas

1 tsp lemon juice

1 small carton crème fraîche

1 small piece plain chocolate

Index